Drunk

in the

Woods

DRUNK

IN THE

WOODS

TONY WHEDON

GREEN WRITERS PRESS

Brattleboro, Vermont

Printed in the United States

10 9 8 7 6 5 4 3 2

Green Writers Press is a Vermont-based publisher whose mission
is to spread a message of hope and renewal through the words and
images we publish. Throughout we will adhere to our commitment
to preserving and protecting the natural resources of the earth.
To that end, a percentage of our proceeds will be donated to
environmental activist groups. Green Writers Press gratefully
acknowledges support from individual donors, friends, and readers
to help support the environment and our publishing initiative.

GReen
wrıters
press

Giving Voice to Writers Who Will Make the World a Better Place
Green Writers Press | Brattleboro, Vermont
www.greenwriterspress.com

ISBN: 978-1-7322662-0-9

COVER PHOTO
Evan Leavitt

ACKNOWLEDGMENTS

American Review, "Night Walk"

Best of the Burlington Workshop, "On Happiness"

Brilliant Corners, "Sideman"

Connecticut Review, "Ugly Beauty"

Chariton Review, "Windfall"

Hotel Amerika, "Looking for the Three-Toed Woodpecker"

New Letters, "Drunk in the Woods"

Northwest Review, "Deer Park"

Southern Humanities Review, "Grasshopper," "Hunter's Moon," "Wild Turkeys, Roosting"

Tampa Review, "High Water"

West Branch, "Wild Raspberries"

Western Humanities Review, "Imposters"

Contents

I

Form, Shadow, Spirit   3

Nightwalk   7

Hunter's Moon   21

Wild Turkey's Roosting   39

High Water   51

II

Looking for the Three-Toed Woodpecker   63

Grasshopper   79

Wild Raspberries   101

Drunk in the Woods   113

Ugly Beauty   127

III

Windfall   141

Imposters   157

Deer Park   173

Sideman   187

On Happiness   205

Epilogue: Border Crossing   223

Suzanne

FORM, SHADOW, SPIRIT

◡⟩

I WAS A PERIODIC DRUNK. I spent months, even
years dry, and then I'd go on binges that lasted for
days. My final years drinking were no different
than most drunks. I spent days in blackouts and then
sobered up, only to drink again. In between—there
were lots of in-betweens—I taught writing at a little
college twenty-five miles south of our place. It's
a rough area populated by a few remaining dairy
farmers, ski bums and upstanding citizens of French-
Canadian descent. When I got sober and joined AA,
I came to admire these souls in recovery more than I
can say. I also read the great Classical Chinese poets
who wrote about a kind of self-forgetting enhanced
by alcohol. I was both literally and metaphorically
drunk in the woods, sometimes under the influence,
other times tipsy on nature and the poems I read.

I don't idealize that harsh life, but as I struggled into sobriety I recognized a kinship between myself and those ancient wine-drinking sages. On one level, nothing was more removed from me than the world of political intrigue and exile of the great classical Chinese poets. On another, I was entirely at home with them, especially when I drank.

I arrived in Vermont with naïve notions about how to survive on the land. On the way, I learned some hard lessons: maybe the kitchen hand pump would freeze up in a cold snap, or we'd have a terrifying chimney fire and had to put it out—or I'd go out on an impulsive drunk (they were always impulsive) that made our survival at thirty below even more problematic.

I have no idea how I kept my teaching gig those drinking years, or why Suzanne stayed with me. Maybe a spiritual path kept us together; for sure we loved each other. She'd been trained as a social worker, but when we came to Vermont from five years of freelance writing in Europe, she ended up working at a local dairy farm across the mountains from our house. She labored alone milking a hundred cows and wrote about that life in rich, concrete detail while I worked in restaurants and taught part-time and scribbled poems.

Back then, I was a hermit drinker. We raised much of our own food, cut our own firewood; we were "good stewards of the environment," and I saw no separation between my drinking and my spiritual life.

But as I grew older, I saw that these two modes of consciousness were irreconcilable.

Still there were incomparably blissful, lonely moments, like this one expressed by the T'ang Dynasty poet Li Po:

Amidst the flowers a jug of wine,
I pour alone lacking companionship.
So raising the cup I invite the Moon,
Then turn to my shadow which makes three of us.
Because the Moon does not know how to drink,
My shadow merely follows the movement of my body.
The moon has brought the shadow to keep me company
    a while,
The practice of mirth should keep pace with spring.
I start a song and the moon begins to reel,
I rise and dance and the shadow moves grotesquely.
While I'm still conscious let's rejoice with one another,
After I'm drunk let each one go his way.
Let us bind ourselves forever for passionless journeyings.
Let us swear to meet again far in the Milky Way

"Amidst the Flowers a Jug of Wine" is both a celebration of and a lament for Spring. While in spots the poem borders on being maudlin, Li Po has great fun at the expense of himself when he tells us in his startling non sequitur, "Because the Moon does not know how to drink/my shadow merely follows the movement of my body."

Unlike his more passive T'ang Dynasty contemporaries, Li rejects the style of much traditional Chinese poetry, where wine drinking is done in serene contemplation with a friend. He's not just tipsy, he's whooping-fall-down drunk. There's no friend here, but he turns his own shadow into one. His last two lines move me beyond the moon and flower into a "passionless journeying," a phrase that puts me into an icy, depersonalized space where the poet and his shadow companion meet again.

For the T'aoist Chinese, the self was divided into Form, Shadow and Spirit. Shadow being an alter ego to Form, and Spirit changing into a Self that travels beyond life and death, "Amidst Flowers a Jug of Wine" suggests Form and Shadow will merge beyond their dualities "far (out) in the Milky Way."

Li might well have intended the poem to be danced and sung by a single performer chasing his own shadow across a moonlit landscape, one I have no trouble being part of. For years, I was bedeviled by my shadow. I chased it through the hemlock woods behind our cabin and never caught up with him.

My life changed in recovery. I've experienced a natural kinship with the woods and have found relief from the shadows of the past. I hope these essays express the naturally inebriated state of consciousness living in the woods provides. They are about a borderland existence, the marginal life between the pastoral and the wild, and the shaky peripheries of sobriety and drunkenness. They're about people, too—a marvelous assortment of souls who've helped keep me sober all these years.

NIGHTWALK

⌒

WHEN YOU FIRST come into the country
after dark, you barely see the shape of
your hand before your face. If there's a
little light, and usually there is, it's afterglow, the idea
of light, or just maybe the remnants of evening. Once
you thought darkness was the absence of light, the
absolute zero of the visible, but now you know it's
void and full, the presence of absence: you turn the
lights back on, but it grows darker still, night rumbles
up through the willows and you are so new to this
you can't make out the deeper patches of darkness,
can't see the place where it all begins.

You have lived so long in the city that even
if you were to see the night sky, you'd be clueless:
Cassiopeia, Orion, the Dippers, the effulgence of

constellations—all this, including the occasional entry of UFOs into the little valley, would make no sense at all. But it's easier to study the night sky than to be immersed in a blank, a nullity.

There's diurnal rhythms, nocturnal rhythms—and less obvious changes in temperament are affected by light and weather. You live here long enough, little physical and mental changes crop up: a thickening of the torso, skin darkening—that ruddy "rustic look"—and the hair coarsens. Your manners are the first to slip: the voice deepens, gestures get jerky; eating with others is a bother (not to smack one's lips or eat too fast).

Too many years in the woods turns you in past the face in the mirror, the ticks and quirks from squinting in the half-dark; and a gnawing lack of self-consciousness comes with years of self-scrutiny: nothing belongs to you, the "I," it all falls into categories of "out there," "in here;" there is time—garden time, firewood time—night and day time. But time's more a texture out here, a quality of light, than a measured space, just as the ephemeral "I" is a rough estimate, a quality of taste or smell: pity the poor hermit whose "I" is as much what others think of him as it is something the "I" designed itself. (That's why organized religion frowns on hermits whose lack of boundaries is contrived by those who haven't lived alone in the woods as a kind of "egolessness.")

For years we lived as though in a trance: at thirty below, we trekked at night to the outhouse, but neither of us resented it: the frosty star-spackled sky, the old-woman yowl of a bobcat filling those silences. At dawn your feet stomping across an icy floor to crank up the wood stove and gaze out the window to the spitty snow; and then in spring the slow painful burst of green, the suffocating darkness coming out of the thickets, and last humps of snow when the world beyond the hollow is alive with light.

Once at dusk, my wife and I got lost on the way back to our cabin from the garden; we knew the trail well—for years we'd travelled it, but losing our internal compasses this time, we found ourselves crashing around in undergrowth, bumping into trees. Funny how quickly the world blurred, how isolated forms—a jagged stump, a stone wall—slipped out of focus: as we staggered deeper into the woods, a sliver of moon rose. Maybe just beyond the moon, where bats dive in the rising dusk, maybe just before our faces—a crumb-trail or a handful of pebbles catching faint moonlight—I thought we'd find our way home though the moonlight drew us further away from home. Surely . . . we'd been this way so many times before, but something about the quality of light had thrown us off-balance.

By this time my wife and I had lived in the deep woods for many years, and most of the time we lived in the half-dark. Our kerosene and gas lamps brightened a few square feet of reading space; when we moved out of their dim penumbra, we were in darkness. In summer, broad, leafy maples hid our cabin;

in winter, hemlocks and tall pines played murky
shadows on its windows.

While we have twice as many sunlit hours in summer as winter, our short winter days are filled with a
brilliant snow-light.

In summer at about nine o'clock, the sun splashes
into a high kitchen window, setting fire to the roof
beams and the rafters before it climbs into the maples;
in winter, the sun is no more than an ember behind
blue hills and sentinel pines.

Too much darkness throws many folks into depression, but to us the long winter night's a welcome
change from a busy summer: to bed early, up at first
light, attuned to seasonal rhythms, for a long time we
lived much like animals. We slept in a loft beneath our
cabin roof and through a gabled window felt close to
the night sky. I remember the first night we spent in
the cabin, when skunks who'd made a home beneath
our cabin were clearing out—it sounded like they
were actually moving furniture, they were so noisy.
The irate racket of them vacating the premises was
accompanied by their bitter musky smell. From time
to time that sleepless night, I'd throw my flashlight
beam across the yard to catch a gleaming white stripe
and the glint of skunky eyes: over the years we'd learn
to distinguish the various night sounds—the most
terrifying, the scream of the brook flooding our yard,
threatening to wash away our cabin; and then there
were the brutal winter sounds of trees cracking at
five in the morning, or the midnight moaning of the
summer bears sick on too many blackberries.

Those first years in the cabin, I developed early morning insomnia. After hours waiting to fall back to sleep, I coped by reading or writing: many of those early mornings I coaxed the sun up by imagining our old road through an alder swamp. Big creepy maples—a few yellow leaves on the beeches late in winter. Cabin in the hollow where the road goes uphill. A few chickens scraping around in the late-March sunlight. And then more silence, days of it, days on end, an eerie dark silence in a dusk that doesn't fall, but emerges from the hollows, the dark wet riverbanks, the mounded snow.

⌒

Years ago, in a forty-below cold snap, we moved our goat suffering from mastitis into the kitchen for a few nights. We've also kept convalescing geese and chickens in here, who all emit a special broodiness that helps us appreciate the healing darkness. Our gander honked peevishly when he was sick out on our porch and we kept on the light too long. I thought he needed more sleep than we did, but when I looked out at him, he stood at full alert, peering through the porch door into the dark sky.

There comes a time each year when I need the dark—just as in late winter, I'm anxious for long summer days, I'm glad for the arrival of autumn dusk. With the coming of dark, I am nervous and mournful; when the night sky becomes more visible, I can walk our quarter-mile road guided by the dimness above the bare maples. About midway through

January, something in the texture of the darkness lifts and lightens. I thought the increasing light affected a mood change in me, but after the return of bitter cold, I knew it signaled a relinquishment of hope that there'd be an improvement in the weather; now the shadows deepen and the snow drifts higher around the windows. A friend from a nearby village tells me he and his neighbors saw three space-ships emerge from nearby mountains, huge floating blobs with windows on the bottom of each craft casting half-acre squares of light on the ground: our county leads the state in UFOs—it also has Vermont's highest alcoholism rate. But we're also night walkers and sky watchers.

Once on a nightwalk up our dirt road, a shooting star lit the way, a blue-white streamer. A moment after the light dissolved into the snow, I heard a coyote howling off somewhere.

Three o'clock in the morning's supposed to be the most spiritual time of the night. Most deaths in hospitals occur at four, the best time for the soul to leave the body. The only certifiably mystical experience I've had occurred one night after I'd been unable to sleep for several days: I'd been reading the Bible when, for a few seconds, I heard the voices of what I was sure were angels singing through the cabin window. When I told a therapist friend about those voices, she said I need not worry about my sanity if I only heard them once.

There's another irony writ large into what appears the darkness's silence since most animals and spirits awake at dusk and are most active at night. My own nocturnal ramblings—physical and mental—begin when I awaken, insomniac, at three a.m. When I first began waking up early, I'd lie in bed waiting to go back to sleep. It seemed wrong to be up and about while the rest of the world slept: I realized the rest of the world wasn't asleep, that daytime was for the diurnal birds. I like best the darkest hour when the dream I've had still lingers and I think of a swamp not far away burping blips of methane light said to be the souls of animals. I think of waking up at four a.m. in my childhood bed, a foghorn hooting on the Sound, the clink of milk bottles; the sputter of rain against a screened window.

My mother taught me not to be afraid of darkness. Because she was projecting in me a fear she'd had since childhood, her over-compensation made me both distrust and like the dark. Born into a New Orleans Catholicism—a Creole Catholicism with more than a touch of voodoo in it—my mother's fear emerged in her drawings of crepuscular bayous and shadowy French Quarter alleyways. For her—and for most of us—darkness meant morbid silence; light meant a cheerful, if frivolous, noisiness. Particles of light emit a kind of ultra-frequency noise you can't hear until you've spent years in the dark woods. I knew nothing of real silence until I experienced the complete darkness of a moonless Vermont night.

One such night a few years ago, my dog Nana and I headed up along a meadow when she caught her paw in an animal trap. A skittish dog anyway, now she was beside herself, and when I leaned down to pry open the trap's jaws, she bit me. I tried again; again she sunk her teeth into my hand, and I had to leave her and walk back to the cabin to get Suzanne so that she could hold the dog while I had both hands free to snap open the trap. But there are other more metaphysical snares for the nightwalker. Alone in the woods, I fall prey to an early morning solipsism. I slip into this state in stages—first with the uncanny sense I'm being watched (I am) by forest creatures; then with the fear I'll meet the ghosts of deceased friends on the trail. I enjoy this fear—it hasn't yet become a phobia. I'm more likely to meet the spirits of Native Americans or early pioneers than I am those of old acquaintances. Then there comes the fear of my own fear—the root of all phobias.

No doubt I'm addicted to being afraid. I seldom take a flashlight when I'm walking the trail. I enjoy the rough gravel, the uncertain feel of it. When my eyes are accustomed to the dark, I know where my fear begins.

Softly, in the sweet opening of dark.

By the crumbling outhouse, or below, in the
    gurgling cistern.

The bat caves. The six-o'clock shadows.

But you can't see them, the shadows, though you feel them, shadows on shadows; you turn over, face the pillow, try to sleep, holding onto a memory of what resembled a face but is now no more than the idea of one imprinted on night sky. It's easy to forget how you came here, how you'd wanted to escape the seething life of well-lighted suburbs, that ordered "illuminated" existence.

Even here there used to be more night light than there is now. But gradually the North Country' has returned to darkness. Used to be you could set your watch by the hoot of the three-a.m. train a few miles away, but now the tracks are a recreational bike trail, and our town clock no longer bongs the hour.

As farmers move out and the pastureland's reclaimed by forest, few lights can be seen from the hills where darkness ripens, flooding the old home-steads, the grown-over gravesites: no wonder when people visit from the city, they want the lights on. Reasonably, they believe the darkness means them harm, that what they don't see can hurt them. My sister from Manhattan wants all lights on, she thinks darkness breeds a malign night life, and she isn't half-wrong. For example, last night the cat caught a mouse beneath our bed. As I slept the sound merged with my dreams—a soft carpeted sound—and when I awoke, the rustle of her toying with her prey turned into a tearing, rending, chewing sound—a devouring. After the cat had eaten her mouse, I felt her gentle weight next to my feet. I heard her purring.

Now that our house has electricity, sometimes I like to turn all the lights on. With the appliances humming, I pretend I'm living in a city. The City that Never Sleeps. But tonight I light candles. On the floor by a window watching the night sky awash in the aurora borealis, I think of my mother: to commemorate the first anniversary of her death, a few years ago my wife and I and my sister visited her grave in Connecticut. There's something about cemeteries that reminds me of aquariums—or maybe it's the other way round. The one my mother's buried in is pocked by ponds; mossy maples and pines cast over the gravestones submarine shadow. My sister and her husband stayed at the cemetery gates (later she said she saw a ghost, a little girl of around eleven in a blue dress through which the tombstones glimmered) while my wife and I walked up the undulating road and didn't find my mother's grave—though we might have passed it. The ground was splashed with silhouettes of dashing clouds, and from the ponds, I heard the peepers, their voices hollow and despairing. I'm sure my mother forgives me for our midnight visit, though the rest of my family—good, rational agnostics—don't: they're not only averse to talking to spirits, but also to admitting anything out there in the darkness is worth talking to.

What most of us fear in the dark is not that we'll meet up with our dopplegängers, our "shadow selves," our doubles, but the possibility that we are alone. We people the landscape with night spirits, with all manner of apparition, not so much from fear that they are there, but because we need to believe—as do our Northern Vermont UFO fanatics—that something is actually "out there." Never mind that "out there" is an interpenetrating system of hoot-owls and field mice, brook trout and hatching mayflies (or that galaxies of neurons spiderweb our over-active brains): it's the nothing, the awful emptiness beyond the world's turbid actuality, that fascinates and repulses.

And here in the North Country's gathering darkness, that emptiness is more present, more actual, than any place I know.

The early Puritans knew it—and suffered it—and they bolstered a severe unforgiving philosophy around it. Hawthorne and Melville tried to exorcise it from the collective psyche, and failed. But their failure paved the way for a more intractable force to fight against the mystery of darkness: there are few spots even in these north woods where I can go without hearing the drone of a chainsaw, an ATV, a Skidoo, or the whirr of tires on hardtop. And among my nature-loving friends, few households don't raise their own globally-linked voices against the emptiness. The paradox of all this is that their fear of the unknown has directed itself toward the known, and that their fear of emptiness—the possibility of the empty unknown—drives them to erase the known world.

Glancing through nature magazines, I'm surprised at how many environmental essays fill themselves with information, with facts, about nature, and how little time is spent in moment-by-moment observation of their subject. Many of these essays briefly describe a scene—the night sky, a glaciated landscape, the batty behavior of bats—then lurch from an impressionistically framed overview of their subject to the essays' fact-filled body: it's a course that's strong on information, short on patient, natural observation, and betrays a profound disquietude, an uneasiness with sitting still in nature.

Even Thoreau, in his last essays, turned away from the patient stillness of Walden; some readers attribute Thoreau's conversion from poet to naturalist, from philosophizing to cataloging, to a fear that was born from his expedition to Maine's Katahdin, where he glimpsed a Raw Nature, and turned away from it.

A few nights ago, when I heard the *ha-hoo, ha-hooo* of barred owls just returned from the south, I was surprised at how many owl voices answered back and forth. I've had a few unfortunate encounters with owls, and almost reflexively I girded myself, thinking their ghostly voices were meant to warn me of an impending awful something waiting for me—a something that's neither particle nor wave, has no weight or texture. When that something comes it makes little difference; I'll not be prepared for it, just as I wasn't prepared for the darkness even though my mother spent so much energy trying to dispel it.

The last night of her life, she lay in an adjustable hospital bed in the center of my parents' big downstairs living room, surrounded by tubes, pill boxes and medical paraphernalia. She'd lost her voice (her esophagus had collapsed), she could make little more than a hissing sound, and as she shrunk away, her dying took up an immense amount of space. Her medications sat on three bedside tables, pills for her esophagus, her pain. Much of the stuff was duplicated—there were several brands of cotton swabs, salves and ointments; mixing bowls and pestles and powders. An uneaten dinner spoiled on a tray on the coffee table. Art books and sketch pads were piled on the floor. Electrical cords for the microphone she used to amplify her voice, for the telephone—my mother rarely used it now—snaked beneath the bed, and she was wedged between all this, mouth slung open, hair slicked back, and more clutter spread in waves beyond her—a bedpan, diapers, a syringe; more pill boxes, loose cotton balls.

When my mother had been well, she'd never watched TV, but now it and the lights were on all the time: somewhere beneath the covers a portable radio was tuned to all-news radio. Everything surrounding her—all the systems and back-up systems, the tubes and syringes and redundant medicines, and the ever-present lights—denied the ineffable glow of life still in the room and reinforced the sense of her approaching death.

⏤

Cemeteries—dismal, lonely places in the dark—suffer the stigma attached not only to mortuaries, but to the deep woods where a shadow-life goes on in the vernal pools, in the rhapsody of snowmelt and nocturnal gestation. There's energy and light in all this—the light of fungi; the energy freed from the slow decay of organic matter. For the receptive nightwalker, there's also a metaphorical magic brought forth by mulling over so much "dark matter." In the week or so since I began writing this essay, three feet of snow has disappeared—the result of a meteoric temperature rise and a deluging rain. Increasing daylight also drives night-loving spirits like me deeper into the forest, in search of the dark trance of winter.

HUNTER'S MOON

⌒

A GUY'S SHOT a buck back of our house and he's on the phone in the living room, calling his son to help:` "For God's sake, come help me. The damn thing's still alive." Then he heads outside into the rain and stands with his wet, unlighted cigarette, and no doubt he breaks into a cold sweat about the deer he shot that got away. A while later a red truck pulls up just below our house—it's the son of the guy who shot the deer—and the two of them hike into the woods, and soon there's rifle fire where the deer had collapsed in our garden. They've pulled the deer across the ravine. It lies in the road, two-hundred pounds of perfection, neck swollen from the rut. Father and son hoist it into the bed of the truck and are off in a cloud of snow and dust. They've left us a plastic baggie of the deer's liver—five-kilos heavy and bloody in the bag—and it's raining hard by the time the meat's cooked: a handful of flour, pepper and salt, one small green pepper, the deer liver sliced and doused with two cups boiling water and then fried with the bacon grease (add the wine later). After dinner, we go outside to look at the sky, but everything's miserable and wet. I think of the hours spent with you this afternoon chainsawing alders and swamp elm along the brook and the road: I never told you how good you looked sloshing around in oversize boots, that when I wanted to kiss you and you pushed me away, I felt suddenly cut loose. Out on the porch, we watch the moon smudged and streaked by clouds, and I know what it is I've wanted but don't, for the life of me, know how to get. Remember when our house was no more than a one-room cabin, and the squirrels would rustle in the roof, and we could hear a November wind tear through the maples?

Guns leave a sour taste in my mouth. My own uncle—my namesake—shot himself in the mouth with a Colt-.45 pistol when he was twenty-three. My father nearly killed a childhood friend with a loaded .22: the gun went off carelessly and grazed his friend's neck. This spring over in New York State, a father accidentally shot his son and turned the gun on himself. The boy wasn't actually dead, but when he revived and saw his father dead (according to the note he left), he, too, killed himself. Hunting "accidents" up here sometimes aren't accidents, but the result of cabin fever, human rabies. I can't help my own anger when I see an orange hat in the trees or a figure crossing through the pines, or when I hear gunfire. (Hunters leave scent trails even I can smell when the wind is just right. Bitter armpit, hair oil and adrenalin smells. Deer oil and doe-rut stink.) Or when I see an empty deer stand, a salt lick a few yards away where the deer gather, unsuspecting. But what scares me are guys who don't hunt but celebrate in their camps, scoping the woods for fleeting objects, seriously overweight guys with more than a little liquor in them.

It's been a bloody end of the week: two roosters got in a fight and one had his eye plucked out—what a mess, his showy feathers spattered with blood. The other offending rooster was still outside, and he must've gotten eaten, because he didn't come in after dark and we couldn't find him next morning. It didn't bother me much, but for you the dead rooster was just another little tragedy in our catalog of the maimed and slaughtered: you take each death seriously, and these little deaths are inevitable. One of our other neighbors down the road wounded another deer and came by to borrow a flashlight after you went to bed. Timmy said he shot the deer—a spike-horn, sixty or so pounds—where the brook skirts the meadow above our house and they wanted to follow the spore, but they never found the animal—and it doesn't matter since they'll keep hunting anyway. The two men stood in the door and looked around bashfully. Then they were gone, or so we thought till more gunfire and they were back, thanking us (such gentlemen), but sad they hadn't bagged that deer.

Next morning I'm out of the woods and into town for errands. Outside the feed store, a few townies stand smoking in the dirty snow. I pick up chickenfeed and dog food, and then down the block to B & N's Fine Machines, where I'm in the market for a new chainsaw to sink teeth into the beech and maple we've cut on the hill behind our house; something with weight and heft to it, says Jimmy, owner of B & N's, and stomps around in his boots. I can't decide on a saw, but the one he shows me, owned before by a farmer, is about the right size. Jimmy shows me the decompression button, the idling screw, the safety bar and choke. He pulls the cord, and bursting into spluttering life, it's loud and feral and smoky, and we take it outside and let it chew through a block of curly maple. I shut the saw off, lug it back into the store where two other guys have just come in out of the November damp. They buy some chain oil and talk about the land above my house that's been logged and re-logged these past three years, how they heard it's going to be clear-cut. One guy's tall and rangy-looking. The other's short and spiffy in L.L. Bean wool vest and grease-slathered boots. Both are seasonally celebratory, their boozy stink setting my teeth on edge. I rummage around examining chain-sharpeners and splitting awls, breathing in the dusty air, and wait around for Jimmy to help his two customers, who are hot to get up to their camps for deer season. Now the two guys are out the door—this seems to be their morning jaunt's last stop: they've lifted their legs on every hydrant in town and are growling mangy growls, the short guy leaning on the tall one's pickup and the situation seems ready to combust, to go badly out of control. They are, in short, suddenly and inexplicably, ready to kill each other.

⌒

On my WAY home by Belvidere Pond, I saw a "Yukon buck" tall and statue-like at the edge, a rack on him bigger than anything you'd see in the valley. Poof, he was gone. I pulled over to the pond. Yellow scum ice spread out from the coves. A little snow fell. The pond was a lonely place, the dark beeches rising on the high banks. There's no segue between that moment and my memory of awakening ten years ago on the bank of the same pond, where I'd spent much of that spring drinking. I fell asleep and awoke chilled by a sunset that creased the pond's surface and bourboned the tall spruces. Something rustled in the undergrowth. Maybe a loon cried. I took off my clothes and waded in the pond up to my chest, night coming on. Three days later you drove me to Maple Leaf Farm, where

I dried out. Neat end-to-story, except at times like this, when solitude ignites a kind of panic, I retreat to a pond on the edge of winter, stiff wind through the trees blowing me home, where you meet me surrounded by all that early winter quiet, which is even more oppressive in the valley just before it snows.

〜

There's something about heading into the woods I like—the way my breath comes short and my heart pounds, and I like keeping pace with the puppy who's getting a sound education on these endless hikes. I go up and up an old logging road following a little stream east. Then I climb to where the maples give way to big, elephant-skinned trees and to a lookout from where I look down the valley across the river. Here you can listen to the whirr of semis on Route 118 and the buzz of chainsaws, sometimes occasional rifle fire. I turn around and head back. I hear a little strangulated whimper in the woods, and I go up another logging road toward a trailer parked in a temporary hunting camp, and I hear the woman's voice, either climaxing or in pain, I don't know which, and I don't know whether to stay or go. But I see her in a porthole window, and I'm not sure if she sees me. I know she's naked, and I blot out the sight and the thought of her. I like to think of our house down below, deep in hemlocks, the hills and mountains squiggling toward infinity, nothing between us and Canada but one paved road; but incidents like the above in which a human voice—a naked woman's voice—cries out, remind me how provisional our loneliness is. I look for the old bear—I last saw him two years ago—but I never catch even a glimpse, and he was the biggest bear in this valley, and when I get home this morning, I find you outside pounding shingles onto our new shed. The sun's finally come through the hemlocks—a blessing, sun in November, but the sadness of these brief sunlit hours!

I pick up a shovel and dig along the brick path where you wanted me to plant tulips. I set the bulbs in clumps, six inches apart, where the stems will be pointed up when they sprout, and I cover them with leafy dirt; then I pile hay on top of the tulip bed. There's the smell of fresh earth moist in the sun, chicken manure and hay and my own sweat. I sit with you as it gets dark at the kitchen table: a little quiet, you say, is all I ask as more gunshots echo across our valley. I don't tell you about the incident in the woods, that a young woman—what I saw is nothing substantial, a glimpse of face, lamplit against the branches—let out a scream. Next morning I'm up before dawn walking to the deer camp: looks like the trailer's empty so I peer in at a table messy with beer bottles and cartridges, panties hung on a clothesline above an unmade bed, and it begins to snow in earnest. I go down to the river and follow the rows of corn stubble to where the water drops below an iron bridge to an old farmhouse: the little dog runs before me, tail wagging relentlessly as he bounds along a Skidoo trail. We go about a mile looking to cross the river over to the cornfield into the woods toward our house, but the water's deep, last summer's islands have washed away, and I think about a late breakfast, you waiting, though it's not a smile that greets me, but a half-empty coffee mug. I head out again to address the maple that blew down last week. Most of it's rotten. Behind, there's more fallen trees, another blowdown from the autumn storms, and the chainsaw's buzzing and wood chips are flying, and when you appear out of the chicken house, the puppy runs to meet you. The snow's suddenly stopped. How long we stand there talking, I don't remember, but there's a flurry of things on your mind that are overcome by a shrieking of crows preceding another front plowing through the valley, and there's the flap of chickens. And then the storm itself, a ragtag squall, and then a great billowing snow. Inside with the puppy and three cats, we warm at the stove. I tell you about the woman screaming in the trailer. There's hunters who don't hunt, they use it as a reason to drink. And I'm reminded of when I'd find an excuse to hole up in someone's cabin with a bag of beer. For years it went on, years like that—quitting took more years bouncing along my "bottom," seeing my own blood relatives give in to it. I was struck just now by how you exploded with your nervous laugh and then went back out in the snow. It lasted the whole evening.

∽

Four kinds of rifle-fire:
1. The kettle-drum shot, heard as a distant, thunderlike rumble.
2. The cough-shot, expelled or hiccoughed.
3. The door-slamming-shut shot.
4. A shot sounding like it's hitting a living body.

∽

Today—rifle fire that sounds like a drummer's rim-shot, sharp and metallic, carries up the steep walls of our hollow into the hills.

I walk up the path along a deer trail on the cliff's edge, but no human footprints, just deer pellets, tracks of coyote; a snowshoe hare's dolloped body-print; the tracings of shrews and mice in the snow.

Two years ago in late February, we had a deer kill behind our house. That time it was coyotes: a pack of them on the ridge came down to the brook and slaughtered a deer not twenty yards from my study window. I listened to their frantic yips and barks as they fought over the kill, and could hear the deer's high death-whistle. Next morning, what remained of the deer carcass was down on the frozen brook bed, a thigh bone, the forelegs gnawed, almost gone.

∽

A landscape cluttered with shopping malls, decaying farms, and farther off the prairie, the Iowa wastes. It's easy to romanticize the split-levels and ranch

houses where you grew up, and right out of town
the vast car lots, the corn. From a distance, even your
family seems romantic with its hard-work ethic and
immigrant thriftiness, its sullen inwardness. How
little we talk about them. How easy to forget and to
tell ourselves what it was like. Of course, the time is
bleakly romantic, the time separating us from the past:
I remember going to Bishop's cafeteria in Waterloo
with all the aunts and uncles—your father scowled at
me through the cheerless banter, your uncle wheeled
up from the table so drunk your aunt had to drive
home. And then the ride after dinner to see luridly
spectacular Christmas lights on a farmhouse out in the
country. I remember the Christmas night dinners—
your mother served oyster stew. We'd go to the new
church across the park from your house and walk back
in the Iowa cold, and then sit around the table where
nobody dared talk politics—they were all Democrats
save your father, who railed at farmers, trade unions,
welfare, and the government. He cowed all of us into
submission—even your uncles, who were in awe of
him. And so, why should I have liked your family?
Or did I simply abide them? (I so wanted to please
them.) When your father visited us twenty-five years
ago, just after we'd moved into the woods, he was
aghast at how we lived maybe because he was so close,
in his memory, in his blood, to a life like our own on
the edge of a poverty he didn't want you to know; he
remembered the humiliation of being poor in a town
where class was defined by the clothes one wore and
the roughness of one's hands. Why all this nostalgia

for a place I incompletely knew? I can't call that past, your Iowa past, irretrievable, because I never knew it; there's simply nothing to look back on. But it is as accessible to me as any of the books on the night table, a past that I've known through you, that I've seen you forgetting. Everyone in that family—in most families, I suppose—was driven to create a world that erased the memory of the one before.

↜

While you were in town I continued cutting the small birches and alders below the house. I pulled the slash down past the pond to the brook and stacked the split wood far enough it wouldn't be washed away in the spring flood. The new pond will be below the old one in that low hollow draining the muddy soil around the road. I imagine a shack on an island planted with spruce and pine, high reeds and succulent grasses, ducks taking off in early morning, or in the evening a full and moon rose-colored on the pond's surface. A hermit shack we'd build on an island in our new pond. We'd cover it with scalloped shingles, one window looking out on the bluff. There'd be one shelf with Henry Beston's book on Cape Cod, books on arctic exploration and the *Collected Poems of Elizabeth Bishop*, and Thoreau's last nature journals.

↜

Suddenly, a great weariness. I keep working past the point of tiredness. Birch and poplars have criss-crossed the stream bed, damming the brook where it makes a turn along the high bluffs. I watch the puppy marking his trail into the pines, irrepressibly curious about the rabbit trails and muskrat hollows beneath the stream bank, Red Dog, the perfect recovery dog. I think of a kid I met at Wednesday night AA, just out of jail for breaking probation, who gave the Red Dog the kind of attention only someone in painful withdrawal will give. He'd gone up into the woods and sat in his deer blind with a bag of heroin; stoned for two days in the woods, he aimed his rifle at whatever moved. I would have killed anything, anything, he said, and I knew he meant it.

I've taken to walking on the flats by the river. So little snow this year—the cold waxes and wanes with the moon. Thanksgiving day, I go as far as a farm house on the other side of the river where I can see the clouds scutting the mountaintops into snowy mesas. Today, on my way back to our cabin, I detoured up toward the trailer. It was stone quiet in the pines. Big truck tracks sloshed up through the mud to the clearing. A little snow sifted down: a pickup parked off the road had in fact gone into the ditch, and attempts had been made to push it back onto the road. I could hear a radio inside the trailer and I recognized the song forlorn and lonesome under the morning moon.

At the AA meeting Monday night, there was talk about Joey (not his real name), who'd picked up again after six months sober. He'd been on house arrest six months and had kept himself dry. The word was he'd been drinking and using, had driven a buddy who'd OD'd to St. Ignatius where the guy died. Joey's stories always terrified me. He'd hitchhiked to every state, had been a hobo and had seen guys killed for a bottle of wine. He said that booze was far worse than heroin, and I used to find the stories guys like he told soothing, if only because they made my own drinking seem tame.

A few weeks ago, I dug up a bag of Jerusalem artichokes and stored them in a cool place on the porch. Last night I mixed the sun-chokes and chives in a cabbage salad that went well with the turkey. We've also stored thirty buttercup squash in the pantry alongside pickles, and there's a barrel of apples to be canned, and tobacco dried and hanging from the roof beams. The pantry stoked with provisions—sacks of rice and flour, dried herbs and spices, just-harvested turnips, hanging ears of corn, all burnished in the morning by November light on the broad planking. Outside in the damp, I see through the pantry window a lone rooster pecking around. By the time we've finished our holiday meal, the sun's shining. And what have I to be thankful for? I recall the echo of kids' laughter, the odor of wood smoke, the ammonia of wet-mopped floors of a high school classroom: my first day of substitute teaching fifteen years ago, and I was drunk. I managed to get through the next three periods. At lunch I drove along the river a few miles and looked lonesomely across the water at the opposite shore littered with a huge truck tire and the trunks of uprooted trees, and I flattered myself thinking I could return to the class and act sober. Not long after, I staggered back into class, my eyes drunken slits. I probably terrified the kids with a lecture I gave—I have no idea now on what—and when I leaned in my chair and teetered backward, I'd have shocked them. I heard someone whisper, "He's drunk." Then someone giggled, and the whole class was laughing. At one point, the school principal poked in the door. He gave a high sign to the students—after another burst of laughter from them, one student got up to go to the bathroom and three others followed. Another had fallen asleep. What was my lecture? Was this English or American History? Who was President of Brazil? A bell rang, the students filed out, and I heard locker doors slamming and a girl's laughter. I had no idea if this was Homeroom or Seventh Period. But, indeed, the school was emptying out, a bus rolled down the drive, and then another bell rang—and outside in the parking lot, it was still spring. An explosion of late-blooming daffodils and tulips—rows and rows of them.

꩜

Just east of here as the land flattens, the boreal forest gives way to spruce and hackmatack, and the towns along the two-lane become fewer and poorer, the air quickens with the scent of pine sap. I like to know that a hundred miles north, the Canadian Lynx abide. That not more than a day's drive west, wolves can be heard howling out their loneliness. This swamp country, black fly country—fifteen years ago, only a handful of moose wandered across its frontier. Now, they're more common than deer. Moose have wandered into our valley, too. Long-legged, ungainly and unsmart, sometimes they walk the main street of our town. A few weeks ago, just before hunting season, one lumbered into the local service station, munched the mums planted at the gas-up stand and then sauntered off.

Most of the land in our valley is posted against deer and moose hunters, but it doesn't make a difference. Hunters go where they'll go. A man will cut and slash five acres of softwood to attract deer who like to eat the tender treetops. A man will cut the prettiest trees to have a view of the house of a neighbor he doesn't even like. In the swampy bottoms, there's tamarack and hemlock, a few scraggly spruce, much of which in the past few months have been cut and dragged with skidders to a landing at the edge of a meadow. Used to be I'd go up to a hollow where the land drains to a shallow pond—more a swamp than a pond—and I'd always see a deer or two, but now that hollow's been sawed down on three sides by Timmy's uncle, who's in the land business and is clear-cutting ten acres to sell as plots for house-builders. Impossible to walk into the swamp without stumbling and falling over downed trees. Or to walk a once-boundary-less land and not hear gunshots. Chickadees follow me along the logging road. There's a pileated woodpecker off somewhere drilling away. Pine siskins. Crows dark and dismal.

There's three types of deer-kill:
1. The clean shot—straight through the heart or juggler.
2. The disemboweling shot (need not be described, but the deer will drag itself miles, trailing its intestines).
3. The thigh and calf shot, crippling the deer so that it can be killed cleanly.

Impossible not to suspect one is being followed, not only by chickadees, but by coyotes who are also attracted to these land-kills and leave ropey, deer-hair scat in the new snow.

⤺

Almost warm by late afternoon. Down in the hollow listening to the wind, I smell the sour-sweet of late-autumn. I walk with the puppy up through dark pines to the last of the old farmsteads. Though regular deer season's over for three days, there's still a week of musket-loader hunting. In the new snow: hunter's footprints, spent cartridges beneath a deer stand at the crest of North Hill. Two ridges over, beyond the brook and a hay meadow, is where I heard the howling woman. There's still much wind from the south. Clouds pouring over the higher range—Jay Peak and Little Jay and Haystack in boiling clouds, and to my right, a leafless hardwood canopy—cherry trees descending to the thick conifers, the alder swamp below our cabin.

⌒

Books pile up around the kitchen, a slurry of half-read novels. We read while we eat. And then late at night to the ting of snow grains on the steel roof. Some moments in the dark sound like a bell tone, pure and unalterable. But thoughts roll in, flicker up from the page: your mother in her hospital bed in Waterloo, folded into herself like a collapsible doll, your brother fly fishing in the Cedar River, his line whipping back and forth in the autumn air.

When I wake, you're outside opening the sheds. The dog and I go out to greet you. You've already cleaned out the pens, hauled hay from the truck to the barn. A few leaves skate across the pond. I take a half-bucket of grain and feed the fish—quickly they rise to the surface. And then back to the house, hearing your soft laugh at the puppy dancing around us.

As I make my way this morning up the same road I've been walking twenty-odd years, it's not impossible to imagine an anger that boils up from no place, steams the windows in a trailer where, after a case of beer is drunk, someone talks nasty. An anger that has no referent other than itself; hidden from the world and thickening, deepening in the woods' silence. Self-devouring. An anger that stems not from ignorance, but from the most desperate sort of self-knowledge.

An anger that burrows into the conduits, addles the common sense (what's left of it), and threatens to swallow it all up: a life, two lives, conditioned, finally, into easy rhythms of wind and stillness.

Fortunately, providentially, I've left that anger all behind.

The trailer where I heard the howling woman is empty: a back hoe and a bulldozer parked out in the open on a rise of land. As I turn down the hill, having satisfied whatever drove me to look again, I meet three kids coming out of the woods all dressed in plump snow-machine outfits. They salute me in French. "*Bonjour!*" And I wonder what relation they are to the trailer—is the woman their mom? It's dark by the time I get home. Outside the temperature's dropping. A Hunter's Moon barely shines through the hemlocks onto the frozen ground.

WILD TURKEY'S ROOSTING

∽

THE TURKEYS ARE BACK. I saw six sets of prints crosshatching the fresh snow this morning. They're methodical tracks; each bird keeps a short distance from its neighbor as it marches in a kind of color-guard formation, big triple-toed reptilian feet etched into hillside. I'm not so much interested in where these birds are going as I am in how their tracks scrawl patterns in the fresh snow on a late winter morning like this one.

Wild turkeys have had an easy time of it this year as we haven't had much cold weather. Which isn't to say the winter hasn't been a long one. Our first snows of early November stayed through January's savage ice storm and our extended February thaw. But despite the warm winter, the deer in our Vermont valley have suffered because the snow's so deep and crusty. Most of our two and a half feet of snow's left over from early winter, and deer have a rough time punching through the crust to the grass beneath.

Because it's been warm, lots of normally hibernating animals are out and about. There's fresh bear scratchings on beech trees—bears love beech trees—and the old snow, until a recent storm, recorded the awakenings of winter sleepers: along the Trout River, the paths of coon, river otter, mink, coyote and deer intersect with beaver and muskrat; and farther in the woods, I come on a big pile of porcupine scat. (Porcupine, invulnerable to predators, or so they think, leave a winter's worth of shit in one dump anywhere, even along well-traveled trails.)

Tracks are abundant along the river, especially coyote whose paths parallel and intersect those of deer, snowshoe hare and squirrel; the pack dens up on the far side of the river in ledges that abut a sliver of cornfield on the narrow valley floor. I heard them yipping and howling early this morning, but mostly I see their paw marks, claws out, a long straight gait purposeful in the snow, or I sense them in woods alongside the river: there's no bounty on coyote, but with open season year round it's not uncommon to see a handsome forty-pound carcass swinging from a tree in our neighbors' front yard.

Yesterday, in the fresh six inches of snow, I found fisher tracks on the dirt road down to our chicken coop. The fisher cat, an oversized member of the weasel family resembling a marten until recently considered "endangered" in Vermont, has a parallel track, front and rear feet, respectively, close together in the snow. Though sizable animals, they range over twenty pounds. They also climb and travel through trees: the tracks disappear when they arrive at the pine and hemlock around our outbuildings. I'm not overly concerned about them hunting our chickens with two huge watch geese who keep predators away, but I've heard stories of emboldened fishers actually attacking and seizing house cats from front porches in our valley.

Tracks tell stories of animals hunting or being hunted, and so when I see those fisher tracks heading toward our chicken coop, I suppress a little shudder. If animal tracks swerve, there's got to be a reason behind their swerving: still I can't not imagine the occasional meandering coyote track in the cornfield along the river doesn't represent a fellow out for his morning jaunt, sniffing, even ruminating, leaving scent trails, catching scent trails.

Tracks leave much to the imagination. There's no way not to project into them my own little fears, to read in their scrim a narrative when they come to the river and disappear across fresh ice where there's no snow, or when at a wash of open water, they dissolve and reappear at the opposite bank.

Like maps and fossils, tracks are more an idea than something real and tangible. Their imprint is not unlike an image of naked branches against winter sky, but when the snow warms and melts, these squibs, blips and fizzles expand three times their size.

Would-be readers of tracks ought to know the difference between imagination and intuition. My imagination breeds tall tales and hunter's hyperbole. Leading me to make of oversized bobcat's tracks in old snow a lion's footprints, my imagination fills the blanks with ghostly shapes in winter darkness and causes me to shiver at the prospect of things unknown in the trees along our meadow.

While my imagination comes from too much thinking, intuition arrives from a stilled mind and stimulated senses. Of course intuition's bred from experience, or more accurately from the sifting of experiences in the woods. But I'm not a "tracker"— that term word implies a predatory subtext to my wandering. I'm not so much interested in the animal as in the scribbling he's left behind. A scribbling that denies a hunter his requisite hyperbole, animal tracks suggest understated grace even when they're deer tracks plunging through bauchy snow. I won't press this literary analogy but to say that vanishing tracks and their reappearance on the far side of open water, or where the snow softens in afternoon sun, mirror the elisions, erasures and whitespaces of elusive prose. To appreciate animal tracks one has to muster an interest in how tracks reflect the depth and texture of snow, the time elapsed since they were made, the weather yesterday or an hour ago, or the movement of the animal.

Tracks draw stories on the snow's undulating canvas: even when the land's flat, snow buckles and strains, powdery one hour, elusively slippery or grainy the next. In fresh snow, one can catch the tail drag of an ermine or fisher, the hoof-skimming gait of a deer on the run: it's said deer re-track old trails, stepping where they've stepped before. Mink and river otter slide recreationally on the meadow hillside by the Trout River, reusing old slide trails until they're deep furrows, just as I ski on my old tracks.

I've followed a bobcat's round, clawless tracks a mile or so as they appeared to follow a snowshoe hare; finally and unaccountably, the hare veered off and disappeared into deep snow, while the bobcat's tracks ended at the base of a big spruce. I don't know (though I would, were I an experienced tracker) what time elapsed between the hare and bobcat, but pursuit implies the bobcat had the hare's direct scent in her nostrils, or that she saw the hare in front of her, or that she followed the hare's scent from where it brushed against trees and bushes. And while those tracks implied the bobcat followed the idea of the hare through the woods, it's also dimly possible the two sets of tracks had nothing to do with each other. Once I followed a leisurely jogging bobcat a quarter mile down a logging road: when she finally reached an open meadow, she shifted from a loping run, and zigzagged and bobbed through the tall grass into the woods.

⌒

An occasional moose ambles casually, imperturbably into all this, its huge hoofs grooving lobe-like notches in the snow. Sometimes I'll come on deposits of moose dung on the hill above our house, but moose are relatively recent in our valley: our game warden says they precede wolves, who will follow the moose into Vermont from Canada. Two loggers I know swear they've seen wolves in the Cold Hollow Mountains a few miles away. Occasionally, when I've heard a howl coming from deep woods, a lower, more mournful howl than anything a coyote conjures, I wonder if the wolves aren't already here.

Those turkeys are also new arrivals: our big flock of wild ones—I've seen thirteen strutting in our yard, the largest, fattest Tom in the lead, a remaining twelve apostles flanking him on either side like a congregation of gossipy churchgoers. Their gobble-gobbles are censorious. Their hooded ruffs resemble the collars of Puritan preachers. Covering the entire valley in a season, they move like minesweepers across the small flat of our hollow in an afternoon. A New England bird, they're dour and industrious, thrifty in the way they'll mow through a cornfield or the broom and mast of an un-mowed meadow. Their quirky, nervous tracks quilt the entire flat of our hollow, sweeping from hillside to brook and back again.

Here's a poem I wrote about turkeys:

Before I could finish a sentence had
there been one I heard
the sound of wings, a burst through
foliage, above & to the right
at the hill's crest, & then the birds's body,
too heavy to be a hawk,
I swear it had haunches, was bomber-shaped
    riding ponderously in the November
silence higher than I'd thought
possible

into the afternoon light,
    high as its heft would let it

    the wingburst heavy, clumsy,
long gone by the time I reached
a clearing where months before a logger laid down
deep skidder tracks. Then
it was gone, & a silence fell, rained
through hemlock,
the shadows of dusk flowing uphill
inky rivulets that reached

    the tornout stumps & hilltop blowdowns
not much later:
and then I heard the birds

six, seven more at roost (in the high, thin branches)

& saw their crooked necks vulture necks
and them peering down at me, grim, pilgrimlike,
& I recognized their shape
& knew a name for it.

~

A few years ago in late March, I followed deer tracks
up to a clearing above our cabin. I came on a freshly
killed yearling, still warm, ribcage plucked clean by
coyotes, an assemblage of bone and gristle around
which new snow tumbled, a snow so fresh only cross-
hatchings, delicate crow prints, remained. Somehow,
I got up courage to see past the hints of blood, the
tattered spoor, a lesson: not of mortality, but of the
brute force behind that hunger, the scattered bird
droppings, the yearling a cleaned carcass. In the dull
winter light, the sequences of the kill were screened
under dustings of new snow.

The forensic facts: a clean-picked yearling now no
more than thigh and leg bones, spatterings of blood
and hair, some barely visible coyote tracks fading
into woods, crow prints so fresh the falling snow
had not yet covered them. I could hear the crows
(they'd arrived back for spring a month ago from
Lake Champlain) as steam rose from the snow. Had I
come on a similar killing scene later that Spring, with
the snow gone and tatters of bloody hide and flesh
scattered in the bushes, it would have been mayhem;
what struck me now was the economy of the scene,
its fragile delicacy.

⌒

Our hollow has been carved out of a glacial anomaly called a "kame." A brook runs through it, forming a sort of moat around our house and further separating us from intruders. Though there's a state road on the far side of our property, we're effectively sealed off by a ridge, a brook, the snowy conifers muffling even the sound of animals.

Instead of looking to the horizon, we either glance up or down to the snow at mole furrows and frumpy snowshoe hare tracks, and nearer to the house, toward the helter-skelter of our chickens and geese. Snow falling from late October to April, a late February snow that veils the awakening of coons who last night clanged the tin roof of the woodshed and overturned garbage; a snow like warm rain, dimming the night sounds, deer hoofs in the snowcrust, or coyotes so close I've counted six plangently yipping voices.

Here in a hollow so many years, I've developed a somewhat skewed view of things. My "horizons" are limited; my perspective's vertical, not horizontal. My wife says I've always had a trusting nature; yet I feel two decades of life here causes me to be wary of strangers. The tracks I leave are no doubt well-sniffed and notorious. I have no tall tale about any animal tracking me, but I'm sure they do, that in an olfactory way they know me more intimately than I know myself. I wonder if animals smell the quality of my gait, not just the fretting I bring from cabin fever, but the way I lean on one foot more than the other, how one of my ankles was broken in a fall years ago, how my scruffy shuffling mirrors my own inherent uneasiness, the disease of being human.

The disease of which I speak I've come by over the years as a means of self-protection. To feel safe in one's skin, some boundaries shouldn't be hazarded. How do coyotes know when the river ice is strong enough to bear their weight in a crossing?

And why do I avoid certain places? What tells me to avoid this, to seek out that in my rambles? I walk the woods this afternoon looking for deer kill. I avoid a certain spot where our brook turns into the gloomy hemlocks, listen for the crunch of the early ice breakup, for the wind shifting to the south; and in three weeks, after the snow's gone and the trout lilies are up, I'll follow the last snow up to the high ledges. But I need to be wary, at times, even of my own footprints. For years I've been tracking myself. Nothing escapes me, everything is tealeaves and revelation: I watch Haystack and Burnt Mountain fall into cloud shadow and listen to the brook below broken ice. After a light snow, I watch old tracks fade beneath a freshly primed canvas and the new snow play tricks on what would otherwise seem obvious. Mud embedded tracks rise to the surface, and there: a disintegrating orchard, five apple trees framing a chapel between tall pines; there: fresh bear scratchings on an old beech. When I last saw him up here a few years ago, the apple trees stood in a wider clearing, but now saplings and pucker bush grow to the brook's edge.

I come to the source of our brook beneath a big hemlock, the water easy and clear with two sluggish brook trout, brown as rocks in the pool, idling. It's April. The tracks fade into a thatch of trout lilies, bursts of spring beauties and trillium.

For sure, I'm being watched. Monitored. Tracked. There's outlandish gossip in the woods not only about me, but about my own domestic animals. The last October before the first snows, one of our chicken was taken off by an owl in full daylight. I don't know if Lucille, our little gray bantam, was actually killed by the owl; my wife saw the raccoon sauntering through our yard a few minutes before she glimpsed a limp Lucille in the owl's talons. The owl took off lumberingly; a few yards past the brook she dropped and then retrieved our chicken: it's rare to see a coon in broad daylight: we speculate the coon might have been rabid or that coincidence put her in our yard moments before Lucille was carried off, or that the owl capitalized on the coon's dirty work: a squall of gray feathers just beyond our front porch, more feathers by the brook; the other chickens hiding beneath the porch, under our coop. The sky clouded up and winter arrived with snow beginning to fall only a few hours later.

HIGH WATER

OUR STEEP-WALLED RAVINE on the edge of Vermont's Northeast Kingdom is fed by one of several major streams flowing into the Trout River. To the west our narrow valley opens to the broad reaches of the Champlain basin. On all other sides the valley's surrounded by mountains that rise three to four thousand feet; Jay Peak and its sister peaks of Little Jay, Burnt and Sugar Loaf Mountains form a barrier to the north, while the ridges of Belvidere and the Cold Hollow Mountains cut us off from the South. When cold fronts march in from the Northwest, rain clouds sometimes dam up, and on rare occasions the weather is enhanced by the uplifting mountains. When clouds are captured and locked in place by natural barriers, and if conditions are right, sometimes it snows and snows or rains and rains.

When it floods, there's nowhere for the brook to go but down at a 45-degree angle, tumbling over boulders, scouring gravel. Flowing from snowmelt and a spring a couple of miles above us, Dreamer Brook spirals past abandoned homesteads and skirts a meadow to dive into a ravine before it tumbles by our house. There are a few deep pools, a waterfall or two. Overhangs of big maple and beech shade the brook trout in summer, mossy behemoths I sometimes fish from.

At flood-time the trout in Dreamer Brook hide in eddies behind rocks, surviving—because they have to—in vacuums made by the onrushing waters: after our flood last summer—known hereabouts as "The Five Hundred Year Flood"—the few trout I caught and released again into Dreamer Brook were scarred by what would have been an infernal pounding.

The brook forms a sort of semicircle around our house, a half-moat protecting us from malign forest spirits. When we moved here our house was no more than a one-room cabin. With no electricity or running water until 1990, we depended on the brook for all our water. Throughout the years we've transplanted trout from the brook to our little pond, and for a while, we diverted part of the stream to power a little electric-generating waterwheel and to irrigate a kitchen garden.

The stream actually wants to travel through our yard rather than around it: changes of its course occur over centuries—even decades—just as coastlines vary with shifting beach sand.

At first our brook's will seems arbitrary, whimsical as our frequent Vermont rains, but it doesn't take long to see a pattern in seasonal and annual variations of weather. In March and April, I pay close attention to weather, since these months are the flood months in our valley. This El Nino year's threat of flooding is as high as ever—even with six feet of snow in the mountains, we expect spring soon. Skunks are prowling (the evening air's ripe with their musk) and beneath the remaining ice, our little brook rattles on; a steady rain sloughed down last night—and I suspect yesterday was the last of those bright late winter days before flood season.

Sometime in the night much of the ice went out—not with a crunching whoosh as after a sudden thaw and a quick violent rain, but with a murmur. Now the brook warbles across a gravelly run below our house, belching beneath the ice and rifling into dammed up pools as it enters an alder swamp at the edge of our garden. At noon the sun hazes through the clouds, the wind shifts to northwest, a gray sky sputters sleet against our windows. A sea change in the weather signaling a reprieve also means a return to a winter that never was.

In the little hollow, these sounds magnify and echo—the wind chaperons the brook's guttural bellowing—and you can't tell if you hear wind or water.

Nothing but our mile-wide valley around here is flat; the rest buckles and sprawls, a landscape of open fields, forest and rivers. Each brook in our valley is forged by the rugged landscape—even the meadows cut into Vermont hillsides are attuned to the warped topography. Looking at a map, I see brooks—Alder Brook, Hannah Clark Brook, Jay Brook—spaced at mile-wide intervals, each draining a towering sprawl of mountainside. I've fished all of them, and Dreamer Brook is like no other. Its waterfalls and deep pools, its bouldered conduits, are shaded by conifers and hardwood rising from banks so steep it's unprofitable for them to be logged. You need little imagination to see in these trees' gnarled gesticulations the shapes of animals or people, to imbue in them your own fantasies and anxieties: in summer brook trout hide in the tree-shaded pools and dart out from overhanging banks; their bellies are golden, their backs speckled like trout lilies—their namesake.

Although most of the brooks are untainted by farm runoff, acidity caused by dirty rain from the midwest is so high during Spring that brook trout and the insects and larvae they feed on have diminished. Still, there are some beauties hiding beneath the ferny overhangs. Usually I fish up the brook, hopping boulder to boulder, stopping to cast my line quickly—sometimes into a crevice beneath rocks, or over a waterfall where I let my bait idle into a pool that always has a trout in it.

But how easy, so very easy, it is to forget when the brook flooded over, to slip into complacency, as I do when I sit by my laptop and look out the windows, one facing the brook, the other to the pond, fresh ice skimming its snowy surface. The pond is a home-made one: fifteen years ago an April thaw accompanied by pounding rain filled it to overflowing. The pond was dug out later for dirt and gravel to fill in the gulch furrowed by runoff which had leapt the banks and churned through our yard. I still hear the rain that came before the flood lashing the roof; I hear the thunder and I see the sheet lightning.

My wife was visiting relatives; home alone, I was reading *Anna Karenina*, pondering the fact that earlier in the day—by coincidence, though I can't be sure—I was flagged down on the river highway by a man in a life-vest. There'd been an accident, he shouted, tears staining his cheeks; he asked if I had a shovel—I happened to carry one in the back of my truck—and I followed him down to the Trout River, brown and roily from spring runoff, where another man, blue in the face, dead or unconscious, had been pulled up out of the current and lay in the grass, not breathing.

A handful of others, all in yellow life-vests, hovered around him, their canoes pulled onto the bank—and another small group of canoers, the drowned man's girlfriend among them, stood a few yards away: her lover had been swept from his canoe by low-hanging willows as he rounded a bend. Ironically, his life vest had tangled in the branches, holding him face down in the water. We used the shovel to cut through the willows tangled in his vest, but by the time he'd been rescued, the man—a Quebecois on vacation in Vermont—died from drowning and exposure, although for a moment he emerged from unconsciousness.

Of course the memory of that man stays with me—in dreams, in nightmares, in the image of a singular April day: the first dead man I ever saw who remains a warning that the river isn't the benign spirit I'd like it to be, nor is it a malign man-eating entity; yet I can't help giving it a desire that parodies the worst human desires.

In the mountains surrounding our valley, rapid snowmelt swept down the washes and ravines that afternoon; for a while the beaver ponds along the brooks held firm, to erupt hours later from a driving rain: but such days, commencing so sweetly, have their own design. The onus is on us to see the signs of approaching disaster:

The air's muggy; gnats and stinging flies materialize out of thin air.

There's a pungency to the stillness, a false sense of permanence in all that overripe sweetness.

Part of the overture to all this is a rumble of thunder over the mountains—there's another louder, more plangent drum roll in the near distance. Thoughts drifting, you find yourself unable to stay focused; the world pauses for a deep breath before an inevitable fall-back to winter. Then, there's silence in the bogs and hollows, a silence unbroken until the first, dolloping raindrops.

That evening, when a cold front slid across the mountains, I'd been reading Tolstoy's epic book; I was at the part where he describes a Russian Spring with its impassable muddy roads, and as I read, I was only dimly aware of the rain that now poured down; I felt comforted by the pounding on the roof, lulled into a complacency I feel again as I peer across the drifted yard. I sensed the distant rumble, the moaning—that's the only way to describe it—farther up the mountain where two feet of snow had stayed until that afternoon.

I would like to say events of that day prepared me for what followed, that years living in the woods had given me fair warning. Soon, the stream grew much louder; I went outside to check how far it had risen, and if anything the brook seemed low. Back inside, I drowsed off only to awake to a wild crashing accompanied by roaring water.

Most floods creep up on you gradually. You have time to carry belongings onto the roof, get rescued in the rising current, stack sandbags, build an ark, but I didn't: caused by a natural dam somewhere above our little footbridge, the water—a flash flood!—burst on me so fast there was no time to find a name for it. I went out on the porch and though I could barely see across the yard to our woodshed—the mist steaming off the snowmelt was that thick—I heard rocks clunking somewhere, made out with my flashlight water running across the matted grass. Walking out to the woodshed at the edge of the stream that now flowed through the yard, I saw I was cut off from leaving by the detour the brook had taken into the road. I tried to wade across, but saw the stream already dug a ditch on the far side of our woodshed, turning the small rise where the cabin stood into an island.

I returned to the cabin. I was alarmed, but not very frightened—I had no notion how bad it would actually get until I heard the boulders—real boulders!—thundering through our yard. Past the woodshed, the stream became a raging river sweeping huge rocks past the cabin window. The water now sloshed about chest-level on a nearby tree; although filled with firewood, the shed swayed and shook in the battering. On its roof crouched Maggie, our black and white cat, her terrified yellow eyes caught in the beam of my flashlight.

These are the various sounds I heard that night:

The brook doing its elephant trumpeting.

The sound of trees ripped out by their roots. (Or perhaps they weren't trees, but my imagination giving form to an Abstract Terror.)

When the water rose to the last step before it would enter the cabin, I began moving valuables upstairs into the loft. I brought with me: a portable radio, a loaf of bread, a bottle of water, my chainsaw to cut a hole into the cabin roof (for escape); I left downstairs most of the writing I'd done during the past five years and managed to rescue photographs of our years in the woods—snapshots of our first garden, our goats and our cats. And after I prepared my loft hide-away, I took a stool out on our small porch. I watched the roiling current reach to the top of a garbage can I'd filled with sap from my little maple sugar operation. Only a few feet away, the can wobbled as the little waves struck it; down the yard, the bulk of the water, half-distinguishable from the darkness, tunneled between two hemlocks; the breadth of that river, about twenty yards, had widened before my eyes—I could feel it lapping at the porch.

Living with the brook close-by for twenty years, I'm not always conscious it's there, but when I travel, I know what's missing. The next best thing to carrying a tape of it around, is to call up from memory the moans, the little half-cries after a fresh rain, the lunatic mingling of bullfrogs and spring peepers, a heron at sunrise croaking as it wades into our pond—or the domestic splash of geese diving and honking, sounds that contrast to those of a world broken apart.

There's got to be some truth in the feeling I had that night that the brook exerted its will—a conscious, vengeful will—against me. The mind rebels against the sullen indifference of nature; certainly, I'm more comfortable thinking the flood was part of God's Plan, that I was, if not the center, at least a part of a vast design: I felt the brook wanted me, I thought it finally had me. I watched huge rocks and trees fly by, heard the voracious sound—a sundering, thundering—and I felt the house tremble.

In addition to the death of the man from Quebec, that night a young neighbor of ours was swept away in his car as he drove home from a dance hall a few miles from our home: the Trout River had careened over its banks; there'd been a detour, but the State Highway flagman, distracted by traffic, inadvertently let the young man drive through; next day, after flood waters subsided, his car was found in a cornfield, and further down that same river, a man out fishing in the Missisquoi River, to which the Trout is a tributary, was swept from a canoe to his own watery death.

My fate and the fate of my cabin was more serene. Just before the waters abated, they'd reached the threshold to the cabin, and after they'd gone down somewhat, I scrambled across high ground to safety and slept the night on a neighbor's floor.

Next morning I found the brook had entirely rerouted itself through our yard. Between those twin hemlocks was an eight-foot hole with trout swimming in it.

II

Looking for the
Three-Toed Woodpecker

⌒

S OME OF THE MOST INTRIGUING—if not engag-
ing—literature on birds is about woodpeckers.
Here's Laurence Achilles in 1906 describing the
Three-Toed Woodpecker:

> The parents when feeding their young, usually
> alighted within a space of three feet below the
> hole and never directly at its entrance. They
> would pause here for a moment as though fear-
> ing they were observed by someone. Then they
> would hop up to the hole and look in, anywhere,
> from up to six times, as if accustoming their eyes
> to the darkness. Once in a while grubs could be

seen in their bills, but, from the actions of the birds when feeding their young, they appeared to be regurgitating. During twenty-four hours the female fed the young thirty times, the male twenty-nine times.

This isn't poetry. It's info-gathering, more valuable than poetry for what it tells me that I can't see and wouldn't want to count. If Achilles had written a woodpecker poem, he might've commented on the damp thickness of the swampy air, or murmured about the hectoring buzz of mosquitoes and the lukewarm thermos of whisky he and his companion drank that long summer's night. But birding literature depends on chronology and facts which intrude on our perception of the bird. Achilles continues chronicling the feeding patterns throughout the night until "at four-fifteen in the morning, the young (after a night's sleep) utter a few sleepy 'peeps' and the male alights three feet below the hole at four-fifteen. The young birds hear him alight and commence to chatter." But he doesn't tell us—nor, as a "scientific" data collector, should he—about a deeper sense of the bird. Rather, he contributes to a categorical understanding of Three-Toedness. When I read Achilles' notes on the tree-toed woodpeckers, I feel the impression of facts transmuting into a large, overall impression of woodpeckers, something that's beyond fact, but is still not poetry.

Years ago, while teaching an Art Appreciation

section of a Humanities course, I found myself so caught up in the historical background of artists we were discussing that I missed obvious elements of their paintings. It's not that I didn't see the trees for the forest—like the ship in Brueghel's great Icarus painting, I noticed but didn't assign importance to Daedalus' son plunging into the sea.

In his well-known poem "Musee des Beaux Arts," a meditation on Brueghel's masterpiece, W. H. Auden notices ". . . . how everything turns away

> Quite leisurely from the disaster; the ploughman may
> Have heard the splash, the forsaken cry,
> But for him it was not an important failure; the sun shone
> As it had to on the white legs disappearing into the green
> Water, and the expensive delicate ship that must have seen
> Something amazing, a boy falling out of the sky,
> Had somewhere to get to and sailed calmly on.

My students saw those details freshly, with disarming, sometimes shocking clarity, and by the end of the course, I learned from them not just how to see the centrally (and patently) obvious, but to take note of seemingly unimportant action at a painting's margins.

These days, when I go out birding with my bird watcher friend Jon Z.—who keeps "life lists" and makes cross-country treks to glimpse hawk and snow geese migrations—I sometimes see birds he misses only because I have no idea what I should look for. Like my students, I have no priority list—no agenda. On today's journey, I've brought along with me bug repellent, a Vermont Atlas, a four-wheel drive pickup to manage the washouts of a deeply rutted logging road, and a degree of patience with the guy I've come to rescue after he bottomed out his car last night. Jon's SAAB is down the dirt road where he left it alongside the slough to South America Pond, and we're waiting in the woods for the tow truck to arrive. It's Sunday evening toward five o'clock. Cumulus boils to the south, a whiff of damp through the tamaracks.

I bring with me, too, an awareness of Jon's compromised condition: he just had a prostate operation and was grounded by his doctor.

"I can't believe you drove out here," I say. "In your shape you should be in bed."

"That's easy for you to say." Jon frowns. "I just got to driving around, it was a kind of therapy."

"Lucky you made it out alive—and in one piece."

He raises his binoculars toward a flutter of wings in a balsam fir across the road.

"So what now?

"We wait for the wrecker," Jon says, content to do some birding before the tow truck arrives.

Jon worships Nature. It protects him, he says, from the heartsickness that's dogged him since he quit drinking. (He's one of those who never experienced the self-generating "serenity" of other recovering drunks.) For him, Nature is a distraction, like liquor was a distraction. Today, he and I are deep in the Northeast Kingdom, a few miles from the last town before New Hampshire. Walk fifty yards into the woods without a compass and you're lost; even on one of the logging roads in the taiga—some barely passable, others no more than mud tracks—you'll crack your oil pan and kill your engine, as Jon did yesterday. Is Jon a fool? Was his latest spree a "dry drunk," or the delusional result of the Oxycodone he was taking for the pain from his operation?

His voyage out to the Kingdom to see a spruce grouse (otherwise known as a "fool's grouse") culminated with him being rescued by a fisherman who happened to be on his way out from South America Pond and ended—as AA stories do—at an AA meeting. (The fisherman was, of course, in The Program, and guess where he was going?) Most bird-watcher stereotypes fit Jon. A poet by temperament, a wanderer of the bogs and hollows, he's easily lost in reveries that have less to do with objective science—which he's great at—than with delight in this buggy world.

Last spring in Ecuador, I spotted the rare cloud forest Quetzal: birders spend their lives searching for them. I didn't see just one—I saw scores of brilliant green and crimson Quetzals feasting on green berries in the canopy. My luck's still with me: as we wait for the tow truck, the bird I'm stalking is banging its yellow head into a dead black spruce. It stops a second or two, and then recommences while a few trees away, some boreal chickadees prattle. The woodpecker doesn't just peck, but pauses between rat-a-tats to admire its handiwork, and then scrapes rather than knocks at the bark—a key indicator that what I'm seeing is not a Hairy Woodpecker or the rarer Black-Backed Woodpecker, also known as the Arctic Woodpecker, but the Three-Toed Woodpecker, distinguished by a barred white stripe down its back, and, of course, those three toes, if you can see them: its breeding sites have been spotted just three times in Vermont, and birders have in these parts identified the pecker, himself, five times. Coniferous birds, they abide in the gnatty spruce of the Northeast Kingdom's taiga moose wallows.

To understand the Three-Toed Woodpecker, as spotted by John and me, do I need to know that Jon is a drug and alcohol counselor at a Burlington detox? That the guys he sobers up are always dying on him? And what's the connection between birding and drinking? Both the drinker and the birder venture into the wild and wouldn't stop, even if they wanted to. But birding is a vocation, a calling—a way to organize the feral world—though in the larger scheme, there are no species or subspecies, just birds and wind and sky and spruce: we've got lots of spruce here, and tamarack, white and yellow birch and anything that loves acid soil and eight months of winter, and lots of water oozing up from the subsoil. Plus a fair share of drunks hooting around in pickups, a six pack between their thighs, one eye closed to see the road better.

The Three-Toed is gone.

A light wind from the east worries the trees. Cumulus gone. The sultriness dissipated. We walk along the road past a pond in the deeper woods. Jon's car is on a feeder road on the edge of a non-existent berm; to our left a spruce grouse is trucking along, bird number two on our "life list," accompanied by a fledgling. The mother has no fear, hence her nickname, "Fool's Grouse." We walk companionably alongside the bird. It has no instinct to flee from a clear and present danger; I note her gray and russet plumage shading into the littered forest floor so nicely I blink to assure myself she's there. She weighs no more than three or four pounds, the size and shape of a chicken with a chicken's innocuous sweetness; she's accompanied by only one young one—I'll read later that the spruce grouse hatches from eight to thirteen chicks. Are others tucked away in the underbrush or dead?

⟳

The Quetzal is a gregarious bird. I've sighted scores of them in a tree in Ecuador chirring like squirrels. When alarmed, they scream and fly in electric swoops of color and return to their roosts when you're gone. Quetzals are so bright they light up a tree. When I first saw them, I'd no idea what they were—but I was dazzled. I ran into half-a-dozen North American birders in the cloud-forest—one had been looking for a Quetzal for ten years but still hadn't seen one. I like to think I was privileged to witness that "bird that would rather die than live in captivity" because to me it was just another beautiful creature, not a statistic to be entered in my life-list.

I was in Ecuador to finish a translation of the poetry of Manuel Federico Ponce begun seven years earlier. On this visit, my wife and I rented a house with the poet a couple of hours down from Quito on the Tandayapa, a torrential river that drops into the Andes' western watershed. It rains every day in there: mist boils up from the Pacific to fall on the upper slopes of the most diverse forest in the world. I'd brought no binoculars, no bird book, just a laptop and clothes for a warmer climate.

I see myself sitting on a wide porch that runs around a house in South America, cogitating on a poem by a little known Ecuadoran poet who follows me everywhere I go. My Spanish is not so good that I can understand Ponce's odd, rapid-fire banter: he has a speech impediment and compensates by talking faster than even a native understands. He's a tiny, agitated man with quirky mannerisms and strange eating habits. As he talks his hands move around, his eyes open unblinkably wide, and as I translate he looks anxiously down at my laptop screen on which the words to his poems emerge in a language he doesn't understand:

The tree throws its shadow
onto a three-fold nostalgia.
Today a bird hidden in the past

sings to us its distant colors.
Green the shadow,
green the calm
as if the world was made of tenderness
and frankness
and tranquility.

A feather has sketched the sky,
the only feather of summer, a perfect feather for a
    new verse.
Again, the afternoon
glides through my heart.

Again the sun eternalizes the landscape,
no more than a country of trees
I see it not to write about it,
but to drink it completely.

The afternoon is so close—a perplexed little
    picture—
and then here no more
this glimpse of hillside.

In Spanish, a feather is a *pluma*, as is one's pen.
Indeed, it "sketches the sky." I'm struck by the contrast between the eternalized, sun-soaked landscape
drawn by that feather and the ephemerality of the
bird, leaving us in a "green calm" in which the bird's
image is caught for a moment. I enjoy the poem from
the viewpoint of an "anti-birder," and I like to think

"I see it not to write about it" in my bird book, not to enter it in my "life list," but to "drink it completely." Ponce's poem is apropos for bird watchers. One's bird is seen then gone, leaving a splash, a glimpse of backdrop. But in Ecuador, everything is backdrop.

Foreground is a mere afterthought on endless refractions of green shadow.

The morning when I saw the Quetzals found me on the porch with fat hummingbirds, and blue butterflies, and a poet drifting around. Occasionally, the clouds lifted to reveal craggy hillsides dense with flowering trees, and I heard the far-away roar of the Tandayapa. I looked out to see The Poet standing in the brief sunlight. Bowing to the sun, he clasped his hands in prayer and muttered something I couldn't hear, and disappeared back in the house.

Just then I saw my first Quetzal, a flash of red breast, an afterthought of metallic green wings, below the canopy. I walked down from the porch and up the hill behind the house to a table of land, where I looked down on the valley across the treetops. And then, the tree directly above our house flashed with sunlight and opened like a burst pomegranate. I saw the Quetzals roosting in the high branches and heard their chirring voices. I saw from the hillside above our house an open slash of hillside, clouds dousing the slopes with off-and-on rain and a distant farmer's shed, a plot of sad-looking corn, and a tatter of wild banana trees. And I saw Quetzals, yes, but if I'd had a camera I couldn't photograph them.

Maybe the great photographers and the great photographic painters could come close to capturing the essence of Quetzals, but that seems beside the point when what one does when one hears the Quetzal is look up into a constellation of them, each an indeterminate approximation of the bird itself. Quetzals don't so much flock as they school together. Often described as "resplendent" and "elusive," they occupy narrow niches of cool mountain rain forest, from 5,000 to 8,000 feet, stretching from Peru to Guatemala and Mexico, an area threatened by slash-and-burn agriculture, logging and oil pipelines. The Quetzal and the Three-Toed Woodpecker are knocking their heads against fate in the form of skidders and oil rigs and nature photographers.

But its nerdy birders like absent-minded Jon and crazed poets like Ponce who'll save them.

I've read that the most popular avocation besides gardening is birdwatching, and I don't doubt it. I'm sure every amateur ornithologist brings to the game his own set of compulsions. While some are failed poets and others frustrated scientists, they all feel a sense of amazement at the natural world, if not a sense of religiosity. (As attendance in churches drop, the bird watching rises.) But at this moment, I'm feeling neither poetic nor religious, but impatient with Jon who I bailed out from similar scrapes before. My memory transmitters are working full steam, and my companion is conked out in the shade, a Vermont Atlas folded across his face to keep off the bugs.

I wander down the road.

Early evening mist rises from the beaver pond a hundred yards from Jon's car, and I stop to soak it all in—the sight of twin flycatchers on a dead limb, the scent of stagnant water and the digestive gurgle of a stream emptying from the pond.

One asks why all this richness and fecundity—all this species differentiation and competition and spilling over margins—finally ends in death. The naturalist's task, that of the 19th century-style naturalist and of our contemporary hobbyist-naturalist, is to attend both to listening and questioning, to sift through details, examine data, and then ask a few questions. Trouble is most times there's so much data-garbage coming in that the one question I'd ask gets lost in the noise of crowbars prying off the lid of the factual at the expense of the actual. I've lost sight of the Three-Toed Woodpecker, but now I hear a knocking on something punky.

Thud-thud.

⤚

After I first saw the Quetzals, I walked along a switch-back up the steep slope deeper into the cloud-forest. The branches and lianas hung so low that, in most places, I kept my head down and my eyes pasted to the forest floor. The view under the canopy was microcosmic: a few feet ahead and down to columns of army ants carrying little leaf-parasols, the after-image of the red Quetzals still blazed in my mind, and the words of the poet were left to pixilate on my laptop screen.

The path steepened, the switchbacks got more frequent. At eight in the morning, the birds still made a racket that mixed with the insects' noise. I stopped to regain my breath and heard a rustle. Through the dimness I could see two black birds big as fattened domestic geese. I stood and watched—eight feet away they watched me back—and then one lumbered off. I don't know how it suspended itself in the enclosure. There was hardly room enough to extend its huge wings, but something beyond air (maybe it used the lianas literally to climb above the canopy!) helped it up and out, and then the bird's companion (its mate?) peered back at me and flapped off. I stood there a moment in awe. The trail narrowed and steepened until I came on cleared ground where a cloud of butterflies were drying their wings in the shade, the essence of leafy impermanence.

When later, as I sat with Suzanne and the poet at an eatery in the nearby town and recounted my morning's epiphanies, I knew it was useless. I'd had a vision, the telling of which, as all telling will do, detracted from the experience. Of course, all writers undergo the same disconnect I did in Ecuador. Maybe our enthusiasm for telling our story gets us away from it. Although I didn't take that walk to have an essay rise out of it, telling's what birding's all about; seeing, scribbling and/or telling, to verify the experience, to make of random events a narrative others might understand. But telling is only the first step toward writing about birds. The writer-birder must cleanse himself of psychic excess and engage his subject. Sometimes, my own enthusiasm for birding overruns the act of birding itself, as it did that morning in Ecuador. If that happens when I'm writing, my words tell me more about my romantic temperament than about the object of my enthusiasm.

↩

The AAA truck hasn't arrived: the swamp bugs are buzzing and an evening coolness descends. As Jon and I walk back to my truck, I hear a coon's chit-chit in the muffled shadows. Somewhere, too, the Three-Toed is at it again, knocking and scraping for grubs in the dead spruce; then it too goes quiet and just as we're about to give up the ghost, the tow guy does arrive, accompanied by a woman and a boy: they're all redheads, freckled from too much Vermont sun. Jon fills out Automobile Club forms; registering a polite complaint with the tow truck guy (whose fault, of course, it isn't, as the dispatcher forgot to make the call [the guy says] and, besides, he's got a pretty, redhead wife and a grinning kid along for the Sunday ride). Jon seems in control at last of his life's particulars.

↩

Two weeks have passed since John and I saw the Three-Toed Woodpecker. Late-July in the north country and the gold finches and grosbeaks of early summer have long since deserted our backyard feeder. A heron is fishing our ponds. I bought two decoys to scare them off (territoriality is big among herons) but these facsimiles apparently attract the long-legged birds: some minutes before I sat down to write this, a real-life heron was doing an aggressive heron-dance a few yard from one of the decoys.

Of course, when I got up to scare him off, he was gone.

GRASSHOPPER

⌒

IN THE PAST WEEK I've tried to think less about my friend, and that's as it should be. Despite my involvement in his life, I didn't know him very well; and though I gave him good advice, I may be to blame for whatever happens to him. One version of his story says he killed himself. Another, no less plausible, is he's on the road to someplace where it's warm. One moment I believe he's dead, the next he may be hunkered down under a tarp somewhere, keeping out of the rain. Or maybe he never left Vermont, but is here under our noses, so close we can't see him. He's made a big mess for his friends and the local police, and because he tried to kill himself a few times, maybe he finally did kill himself, and when the ice goes out of the Lamoille River this Spring, his body will be found.

But what interests me are those moments leading up to his disappearance, not his life history.

Begin in a mountain town twenty miles from the Vermont-Canadian border. In the wee hours on an early March Thursday, a young man in a tattered gray coat carrying a walking stick bolts out of his apartment, and glances down to the Mobil station and the stoplight and across to the park. Then he lopes north out of the old part of town up Route 100, past the Bijou Theater and crosses the bridge over a river dam, the voices not far behind. Does he stop at the bridge, does he jump in? No one sees him this early, or if they do, they'll forget him. The police out looking three days later find his wallet and his credit cards, his camping gear, his hats and scarf and sweaters in his apartment. By this time, his body will have swept down the river in the spring rains of the morning after he went missing, or he'll be fifteen miles north in St. Albans, camped out behind the Shopping Center. Seven sightings of him will be reported to police from St. Albans, where his girlfriend has an apartment. But if he's alive, he'll be afraid to be seen, afraid to be alone—and yet afraid to be with people; though he's hungry, he won't eat for fear his food's been poisoned.

If he's eaten by now—a week after his disappearance—it's from the dumpsters.

On Thursday outside Pizza Hut, a guy of his description makes a phone call. The answering machine clicks on; he pauses to hear a familiar voice. Then he returns to the woods behind the mall where he sleeps under a dumpster.

At night he wanders the mall, or circles the block where his girlfriend lives, or wanders disoriented in the marsh behind the mall, or lies in a culvert, decomposing into the melting snow. If he has a sense of time, he knows it's a week since he fled his apartment, driven out by the voices, his only companions, which no longer tell him to kill himself.

Or one morning, he walks the five miles from town to St. Albans Bay where an ice fisherman has seen a young man with scratches on his face in a long gray coat carrying a walking stick. Because people have ingrained in them a way of spotting the mad, the ice fisherman knows the guy with the walking stick is crazy, and he'll also know that he's harmless to everyone but himself and that nothing can be done for him.

In any case, after the flurry of sightings in the first days of his disappearance, there are no reports of him: he may have hitched or walked south—he can't go north unless he passes through Canadian customs, although he could walk unnoticed across the border through the woods. If he's here in the area, the possibilities are endless. The mountains. The lake. The frozen streams and rivers. Death by exposure. Driven to it by voices that aren't voices of God, though God's there beyond a broad valley that opens into stars that he would have seen from where he camped before the cold weather set in.

What kind of a man are we talking about?

Stubborn, self-willed; hardy beyond reasonable outdoors toughness and at the same time susceptible to suggestion; alternately angry and remorseful and used to getting his way, especially when it's clear he won't get it.

And knowledgeable about things like pitching tents and making fires in rainstorms, finding his way up an unmarked trail in darkness, or camping in the dead of winter.

And yet wary and skittish, prone to angry suspicion.

And charmingly vulnerable, attentively childlike.

And impulsive.

God-struck, but not god-drunk.

For a while he came to AA meetings alone, and then in mid-August he began showing up with a woman twenty years older than himself. Soon the two of them were an item, and he, bald-headed and gauntly red-bearded and tall, and she, a nervous little bird with cropped hennaed hair, seemed toxically suited to each other. He needed a sponsor; he wanted the attention of a father figure more than a mentor. I wasn't enthused about sponsoring him, but I ended up doing just that. We spent a few hours doing "The Steps," a long, aggravatingly useful process that focuses on turning over the alcoholic's will to a "higher power." Then he takes a writing class at the college where I teach, and writes a brief essay on his family and drinking that indicates a head not screwed on tight. Mostly he sits at rigid attention and listens to the others, who must sense the strangeness in him. This fall, the Fall of 2001—an extraordinary fall, by any measure— the other students' writing seems as demented as his; there are stories of rapes and decapitations, binge drinking, self-mutilation; and though a few stories are good, my mood's so bleak, I can't see it. My students complain of my unwillingness to accept mayhem in fiction: I'm intolerant, rigid, they say. I read aloud sections from John Gardner's *On Moral Fiction*, putting everybody to sleep when I talk about how character needs to be shaped by ethics, that people on the page are no less real than we are. One afternoon, I look across the classroom as my students blink and doze (outside an early September rain's pounding down).

All, that is, but the young man: he stares at the empty blackboard.

In that moment, a thought strikes me and wings away—it would've come to anyone who knew him even slightly, that someday he might kill himself.

He approaches me in the parking lot after class, and I suggest he write about a less personal subject, that he blend the family stuff into a less autobiographical piece. But he's not listening. Writing fiction's slow, laborious, I tell him, and while a few evening dragonflies drift around after the rain, he tells me about his time ten years ago in a mental hospital and of his career in the military (he was encouraged to become an officer); and about the anger he feels at his father; and of his love of the deep woods. When he remembers the trail, his eyes light up and his voice takes on a Virginia softness. Of course, the trail will be important for him later, as shall his own quest for a solution only an anti-psychotics cocktail can fix.

He'd come to Vermont from Virginia last summer, to find his birth mother. It would have been the first and only contact with her since his adoption thirty-two years ago. Their reunion's a failure: she makes clear after a cordial meeting that she never wants to see him again, but he's very stubborn and unwilling to let things drop, though it's clear in how the woman gently averts her gaze and cuts short their meeting (there are things to attend to, a life to be lived) that she'd like him to leave. The mother in a trailer in a southern part of the state living on a disability check has no interest in her son. There are two other children from other unions, and besides, this new young man, her son whom she's never met till now, seems crazy. Is there a history of mental illness in his family? he wants to know.

After two more trips to visit his mother, he learns she's a Middlebury graduate, that she'd picked up his lawyer father in a Burlington bar, and that there's nothing to be done about the mother, and that his own family, the family that raised him, is the one he's stuck with. But before he lets her go, he returns to her house on his birthday and is even more shaken by her remoteness.

I come into the picture sometime in August. We've known each other a month now, and though

I don't dislike him, he makes me feel claustrophobic: he follows me each night after meetings to my car and hangs onto me as I try to make my get-away. It's not the best moment. I've grown disenchanted with the AA program: one of my sponsees has "gone back out," another uses me more as a therapist than a sponsor, and another's in jail. After years of sobriety, I know I can't counsel anyone on childhood trauma or mental illness; all I'm an expert on is how not to drink. In any case, I hear, blow by blow, each of the young man's disappointments and refer him to a therapist friend of mine. I warn him before he's even contacted his biological mom– as do his other friends—that he ought not invest too much in her.

But I've got my own problems: I'd brought my aging father up to Vermont from Long Island a little more than a year ago and put him in a nearby rest home, where he stayed until March, when he had a fall and suffered a bout of pneumonia. Suzanne and I are both jealous of our time and protective of our solitude and independence. I do my teaching. I write a few hours each day. I like to snowshoe and cross-country ski, and I garden with my wife in the summer. Two days before the 9/11 disaster, our little retriever eats some compost, vomits, and goes into a coma. The dog's hardly breathing, his eyes are turned up in his head, and we spirit him at eighty miles an hour to the vet's, where he revives on the operating table. The next day I drive a completely recovered pooch back home. The car radio is on and tears are streaming down my face from the same shock I see on people's faces along the road.

That night I go to an AA meeting, where the young man's already waiting for me. Notwithstanding my reservations, I like him. He's funny and self-effacing and quirkily brilliant, and both charming and goofy (goofiness is high on my list of estimable qualities). He also seems uninterested in those tragic events— the events of 9/11—unfolding around him. In the parish hall of our local Catholic church, he leans back against the coffee machine and laughs at something I say that's not very funny, and when he turns serious, scratches his beard, runs his hand across his completely bald head, he seems old and not particularly wise. We go outside and he retrieves a scruffy red notebook, his trail diary, from his truck and begins reading from it. It's comically self-deprecating, full of rich detail, and, of course, crazy. He reads until the twilight's gone and darkness plops down—he doesn't seem to know how to stop—and then that same week come his phone calls at six A.M: one day he's depressed, the next he's manic. Other times he chirps away, happy and well-adjusted.

Early October and summer lingers on. He and his girlfriend have been doing lots of hiking and canoe-ing, two idle grasshoppers scraping away on their fiddles before the first killing frost. And then like a door slammed shut, winter blows in, and he's struck by restlessness and leaves the woman. He borrows a teepee from me I've actually never used and asks if he might camp out in the woods behind my house. At this point, my wife puts her foot down. If he gets the teepee he can't live on our land, she says, because she knows what this will lead to.

~

Nothing's to be said for my savior complex. As a kid I felt a kinship with handicapped and mentally disturbed kids—I always had a friend nobody liked, a maimed pet I tried to nurse to health. I may have done more counseling as a teacher than actual teaching. After I joined AA, I twelve-stepped my students. Who knows why I'm like this? When I drank, I was attracted to other drunken misfits who made me feel almost completely normal: my interest in them was humanitarian and literary. I loved a good story, especially if I were part of it. But I don't have enough time or patience for the young man. I rarely see him except outside AA meetings. But he continues to call me his "sponsor," and finally I accept that role. After he disappears, I'll experience the usual denial, anger and guilt (but not acceptance), and—among a few blameless others—I'll blame myself and even AA for what happened.

I guess I cared about him because of his good intentions. At first he seemed to want to get sane and stay sober, to attend meetings and work his program. I felt that his desire to connect with his "higher power" was strong enough to get him through hard times. I liked his contradictions, his dangerous mood swings, his shifting enthusiasms, and I admired his backwoods' self-sufficiency, his lack of pretense. I had in common with him a mistrust of authority. I also shared his impulsiveness, his quick-to-judge impressions of people and situations. But a lot of what I appreciated in him was bound up with what I didn't like and didn't want to know. Soon I became aware of his smoldering anger, his childish rages—last December an AA mechanic friend who works in the local filling station complained to me that the young man had hired him to put chains on his truck (he had no snow tires), and that when he was given the bill, he threw it in the mechanic's face and drove off. He was also a kind of country wastrel and spent a lot of time casting about without purpose. But I never learned much about his drinking history—how much he drank, what prompted him to drink—and I had no sense of how he acquired or kept friends or if he'd had any long-standing relationships with women aside from a last girlfriend.

Finally, what drew me to him was that he was authentic, the real thing; a fellow-sufferer who doubted his own truthfulness. But what's authentic? In his case it was his unwillingness to accept pat answers from anyone. Once during a cigarette break at a meeting, he turned to me and said, "I haven't been honest with you about lots of things."

I paused and looked at him, disturbed by his urgent tone. I realize now that what he was talking about wasn't dishonesty, but his unwillingness to deal with his past.

Sometime in early December, the young man takes himself up Burnt Mountain above Hazen's Notch outside my town. He isn't equipped for the season: he's got a tent, a light sleeping bag, but none of the hi-tech gear campers use these days, and conditions along the border are more severe than what he'd have seen in the Blue Ridge or the Smokey Mountains. He'd gone up there (I voted against it) to make communion (and to escape his girlfriend), and he's willful and stubborn, but when it comes to the woods, he's confident. Although he's trying to detach from his girlfriend, the relationship has got a powerful grip on him. I know the woman from years back, and I wonder if those voices he begins to hear a month later aren't his brain's addled attempt to screen out her voice. But I don't tell him to follow his instincts and make a clean break from her (Later, after he disappears for good, I think, "Discretion, be damned! Did you have any choice but to tell him?").

He stays the better part of a week on Burnt Mountain. It snows very little, just a light dusting, and the clouds shift around: one moment the sky's cobalt and he can see the shoulder of Sugar Loaf and the peaks of Haystack and Belvidere mountains; and another moment he's in a swirling mist. He doesn't venture far from camp, and when fear takes hold, he spends the night in his teal-green truck a quarter-mile from his camp, sleeping very little, and if he's cold, paces outside his tent. He becomes desperately lonely. He finds the beautiful carcass of a coyote and hangs it in a tree.

After he comes down from Burnt Mountain, what began as a spiritual quest the year before on

the Appalachian Trail turns into a struggle to keep
sane. This leads him into some of the sketchier corners
of religious life in the North Country. He spends a
few weekends at the Saint Benoit du Lac Benedictine
Monastery in Quebec, where an old monk punctures
his seriousness by showing him Three Stooges vid-
eos. He attends Abenaki Indian sweat lodges, and is
befriended by a recovering "tribal elder" drunk who
no longer attends AA meetings. The man gives him
a "sacred" walking stick (the only thing he takes from
his apartment that Saturday morning in early March),
instructs him in cleansing rituals and fills the young
man's voice-teeming head with omens and signs.

Throughout the period from late-September till
early January, he holds down two care-giver jobs. He's
got a way with young people and spends three days a
week with two mentally retarded teenagers who love
him to death. He sings and jokes with Dean and Jon,
and drives around listening to country music on the
truck radio, attending hockey games and wrestling
matches. He's also got another job manning the desk
at a local Samaritan House. Though he's dropped my
writing class, because he can't focus long enough to
write, he begins to rely on me for advice only a profes-
sional might give.

∽

Our mountains average about thirty feet of snow each
year. Their summits slice into the jet stream that loops
along New Hampshire and Vermont's border with

Canada, dragging with it storms that last for days. Hikers become disoriented in these storms: during our last unusually mild winter, there were several rescue missions for lost snow-shoers and skiers, and though the highest mountains reach up less than five thousand feet, even in early spring arctic conditions prevail. Not properly dressed, one loses one's head, and gives in to alpine rapture.

I've talked to a few skiers who've been lost in the winter woods—all said that while they know the dangers of cold weather, the temptation's overwhelming to give in to it. I can't think of an easier way to kill yourself. But I've never tried suicide, and I haven't heard voices, save once when I was recovering from a drunk; for no more than a moment I heard them, but they didn't ask me to kill myself like they did to my uncle Roger, who blew his brains out on a New Year's Eve after losing his shirt in a poker game. Actually, I have no idea whether my uncle, for whom I was named (no one's ever called me by my real name) heard voices. But audible or not, there are commanding "presences" that want to do us harm.

When I was in my last year of high school, I read Albert Camus. In his *The Myth of Sysiphus*, Camus says there's only one important philosophical question—whether or not to commit suicide. But I can't believe most people who've killed themselves think of metaphysics when doing it. My interest in suicide was provoked by the void I'd fallen into as a result of my parents' separation. I might have unconsciously thought of ending my own unhappiness, but not having a name for it—depression wasn't a frequently used term those days—I assumed my state of mind was a philosophical one.

Freud uses the Latin word "melancholia" for what we now call depression. It's the bog we slog through when we wander beyond sadness into despair; the blues gone bad; the worst day of your life over and over. And a falling away from God. In *Inferno's* thirteenth canto, Dante turns the Suicides into trees whose leaves are "not green/(but) earth-hued:/No fruit, but poisoned thorns." The first part of his canto is a series of negatives, reinforcing what's been lost, as we're told by one of the inhabitants, through treating the "juster self unjustly." But sometimes when both the ego and the soul can't take it anymore, they do themselves in.

I never understood why Dante—who seems to have compassion for those he's sent to other places in Hell—ignores the souls driven by madness to take their lives (surely such people existed in his day, too). Instead, he connects all suicides with pride, condemns their souls to inhabit lifeless trees whose branches when torn or broken "hiss with escaping air, so that branch flow(s) /With words and blood together." Like Dante, in his Sysiphus essay, Camus ignores the role played in suicide by mental illness. Once I read in a psychology book that "Full blown psychosis comes from disorderly thought impulses," and I imagine the consciousness of a potential suicide is a cacophony of brain static and self-loathing. A common conceit for

the suicide's state of mind is of a no-longer free will
pirated by a super-ego casting itself onto the rocks of
Hell while the soul helplessly watches on. There are
also those who've been driven to it by philosophical
idiocy or metaphysical despair; for political reasons—
or for the glamour of it. History includes Empedocles,
one of the first Greek philosophers, in the idiot's category: Believing that in each successive incarnation
one ascends a ladder from King, to Philosopher and
then to God, Empedocles jumped into Mount Etna,
an act memorialized by Colley Cibher, one of the
worst poets of England's eighteenth century, who
wrote, "And great Empedocles, that noble soul,/
Leapt into Mount Etna and was roasted whole."

Nowhere do I find an account of an animal com-
mitting suicide.

But there are places, like Morrisville, Vermont,
in late-winter, that tempt a half-sane person to it—
cheerless towns whose slushy streets and scruffy front
yards are flanked by low-to-the ground paint-chipped
houses. A boarded-up bait shop, a defunct railroad
trestle (the trains have long stopped passing over it),
and Fred's Fine Furniture (on its last legs now). A run-
down barbershop and a '60s-vintage shopping center
add to its mournfulness. In late-winter, attendance at
AA meetings doubles. An ill wind sweeps down the
hills. And then in mudseason, the redwings flock to
the cedar breaks, and with the sudden bitter promises
of spring, the thoughts of many turn to suicide.

Vermont has the highest per capita rate of suicide
in the U.S., and most of it happens during the "suicide

months" when the sun returns, not in deep winter. A neurologist friend who's studying seasonal affect disorder in Oregon, which has as many cloudy days as Vermont, tells me that the deepest depressions occur on the cusp of seasonal change, in mid-fall and early spring, when bio-rhythms go out of whack.

Why should Empedocles, that fool, leaping into Mount Etna (let's say it's a dismal Sicilian version of an April day in Vermont) seem silly? The "April Fool"—the Fool who rules the Tarot Pack—isn't only a liar, but a trickster, a joker, a sage. He wears odd gaudy hats; he stumps us with riddles and performs the hoodoo of death and rebirth.

What this fool says to us makes sense and is complete nonsense.

↬

The young man's last month or so in Vermont leading up to a first suicide attempt is the story of a life at spiritual cross-purposes. Under the tutelage of his girlfriend, he's introduced to people with names like "Eagle Feather," "Gray Wolf," and "Grand Father" (I met a lot of them when my wife was tribal director of Abenaki social services in Vermont). Some collect disability, others scrape by on part-time jobs, and I don't know if any understand the woods like the young man. One morning, he calls me from a house in the town of Richford that's been turned into a Russian Orthodox "monastery." He's sought advice from the priest, who keeps him up all night chattering about the Virgin Mary and harangues him next morning with a sermon in Russian. Later—same day, new place—there's another call from an Abenaki's home at a sweat-lodge gathering fifty miles away in the Northeast Kingdom. I can hardly hear the young man's voice beneath the television blare and the shouts of children.

And I don't hear from him again for another couple of weeks: he hasn't got a phone in his new apartment (I've still never seen the place, nor do I want to), though I hear from the girlfriend who calls me late at night. She has seen an astrologer, has had her aura doused, and her chakras straightened. Still, her agitation over the young man's mental condition is palpable. "What can we do with him?" she asks.

Then, in early February, he and I have a falling out over his refusal to take his meds, to continue with therapy, and to do his Program. He also knows I disapprove of him quitting a dishwashing job he's just started in Morrisville. These phone chats are slightly reserved assurances he's doing well, or not so well.

I'm not doing very well myself. My eighty-six year old father has to be transferred from his rest home nearby to a nursing facility, as he's lost bladder control and is seriously demented. I drive the old man to a big Gothic mansion called "Red Stone" and sign the papers that admit him, hug him (he's got no idea where he's been taken, much less what day it is, and only a vague idea who I am), and leave him in his new room. On the way home, I think of the young

man and am shot through with premonitions. I try to
erase him from my mind, to do what seems now to be
the unimaginable—THINK POSITIVE. And then a
few hours later a light snow's sifting down, and I'm
sitting over coffee at a local restaurant with James W.,
a good friend from the Program, and I ask him what
it is about AA that drives me nuts and at the same
time brings me a peace not even music can provide?

Toying with an unlit cigarette (he's trying to quit)
for the longest time, he finally says, Well, that's a
hard one, maybe it's the people, not just the ones I
like, because there's guys I try to avoid in AA, but
the crazy things they say that give me a lift. Silly and
inconsequential things like how the cat took a dump
on the kitchen floor and nobody cleaned it up for a
week, or how somebody's wife spent a paycheck on
new curtains and they went hungry for a week. And
James says about the phone call I get in the middle
of the night from some dude who can't sleep and is
thinking about having a drink.

Two days after our mutual friend turned up
missing, James and four local buddies took snow
machines up Burnt Mountain, hoping—and not
hoping—to find our friend. Half-way up the mountain, the trees were so thick they left their Skidoos
behind to hoof it over the stream beds and hummocks and boulders and ice falls; in places, to avoid
slipping, they had to grab hold of saplings and punch
their boots through the crusty snow. Night coming
on, it was cold, but they looked up in the trees (for

hanging bodies), scuffed around in the snow feel like they'd left nothing unturned. But there was nothing, just a gathering darkness, and on their way back, they stumbled down switchbacks along the steep south-face to the road.

〜

While I don't like thinking in huge adolescent generalizations, part of my recurrent depression comes from my uncertainty about essential aspects of life—those same questions that bothered me as a teen have caught up with me. One of the things that moves me about my schizophrenic friend is his search for answers and his earnestness. Is there a pattern to our lives, a reason for suffering? he seems to be asking. Other questions that perhaps only he'd have answers for have come to me through his presence in my life.

〜

What's my responsibility, how far can I permit myself to go, in helping people?

How much am I to blame? Did I make any impact on his life, and—most importantly—did my own rejection of him make a difference? Did I abandon him? And is there a spiritual way out of madness like there is for the "suffering alcoholic"?

I ask these questions not only because of the senselessness of his possible suicide, but from the chance that he's wandering around somewhere completely drunk or crazy.

I'm also struck by how little I really knew him until he'd actually gone—that after he'd begun hearing voices, what kept him sane for brief and less-brief periods, was structure and order and the discipline of hard work. According to his adoptive mother— I met her a few days after his disappearance—since age thirteen he'd had a history of attempted suicides and dramatic disappearances. For ten or so years, he went in and out of recovery programs and mental hospitals; but because the medications left him a drugged-drooling zombie, he'd developed a fear of psychiatrists.

The last time I'll see him is on Valentine's Day, when he visits my office with his girlfriend. He looks pale and shaky, has shaved off his beard. They hug me and hang in my office, rifling through my book-shelf, even though I've got a student waiting to see me and they don't take the cue that I'm busy. He leaves a Valentine card that tells me little of what his state of mind will be like the last weeks he's known to have been in Vermont: I won't quote the card, but he writes with great affection, scolds me for being too somber—"lighten up a little," he says—about my class work, and that he's begun meetings again in Morrisville.

On the Friday of his disappearance at around four in the afternoon, his most recent sponsor knocks at his apartment and hears someone inside. No one comes to the door. It's been warm the past few early March days—the dirt roads are tawny with mud, the cornfields stubbly where snowmelt's drained into the river, but the rain of the night before has turned to a sleety snow. According to the young man's woman friend, he'd been hearing the voices all that week ("Tomorrow, you're going to kill yourself," they say on Tuesday). After his disappearance, she'll find torn-up letters from her and his priest friend in Virginia and other friends in his wastebasket.

All this follows an attempted suicide the Saturday before his disappearance: after arguing with his girl-friend at her apartment, he'd crashed his truck into a boulder along the highway and went to a hospital with only facial cuts and abrasions. The truck was totaled. A resident shrink warned him that he was entering a treacherous period: if he didn't take his meds and submit to psychiatric care, he might not survive the next two weeks. There was no legal way he could've been kept in the hospital. Then he was released, and not a week later he disappeared for what appears to be for good.

When the young man had gone out that last Friday, he'd have passed the town's little library and crossed Route 100 at the Mobil Station, walked along the two blocks of store fronts and the movie theater past an Italian restaurant. If he turned right, he would have crossed the iron bridge over the river; and walking a mile east, he'd have come to a broad, marshy, ice-covered lake. The images that stay with me are of him walking in the rain—of the river and the vague dawn—things I haven't seen as he saw them, but which say that the power of my imagining him is stronger than my memory of him. I walk a kind of grief walk around the cabin. I circumambulate the kitchen table, and with the lights off, the late-winter moon's so bright I can read the titles of cook books. The wood stove spits and crackles, and I think of 19th Japanese Haikuist Issa's poem written on the death of his son:

Oh why did it break
why did the wild pink break?

And there's Issa's less violent poem written just before he died:

A bath when you're born
a bath when you die—how stupid.

WILD RASPBERRIES

⁓

I WALKED UP OUR MEADOW last evening and saw the tiny blooms of raspberries—already weeds had grown up around the old farmstead above our house. Everything's early, trout lilies and trillium up in early April; dandelions early, and fiddleheads exploding so fast all you can do is exclaim before they've gone by. The same with the sun-chokes who've already overtaken the garden, and the lilacs that went crazy two weeks early, as did the apple trees and the jack-in-the pulpits that appeared before mid-May.

I'm so used to cold springs, to the waiting-forever for the first signs of life, that when they come I'm surprised they ever arrived. Sometimes the waiting—in other years when winter goes on and on and we're grateful for even a little sunlight—becomes an end in itself: when fatigue overtakes me, I'm like the subject of an Emily Dickinson poem who gives into

a kind of drugged stupor, "the Languor of (a) Life/
More imminent than Pain..." and I try to shake myself
awake. But as Dickinson says:

> A Drowsiness diffuses   A Dimness like a Fog
> Envelops Consciousness
> As Mists obliterate a Crag –

Even this year I felt that languor—"Pain's Successor,"
Dickinson calls it, though I'm not sure I even knew I'd
experienced the pain, it was so *diffused*. In November,
Sophie, our gray keeshond, died of old age: we buried
her a week after Thanksgiving. In Spring, we marked
her grave by planting daisies and yarrow.

Still, her death lingers. The pain's masked by our
slow, numbed emergence from winter.

Dickinson says later in her poem: "The Surgeon
does not blanch—at pain—/ His Habit is severe—"
and I wonder what surgeon she's referring to. In our
case, it was the veterinarian who paid a house-visit,
administered the shot, put our dog to sleep.

> But tell him that it ceased to feel –
> The Creature lying there –
>
> And he will tell—skill is late –
> A Mightier than He –
> Has ministered before Him –
> There's no vitality –

Says Emily, whose last lines relinquish what dim
awareness her patient still has.

These lines might be read as an understanding of the numbed consciousness of the dying—a page from The Dickinson Book of the Dead; or as a recognition of the death-in-life we go through when grieving. Dickinson's sensibility amazes me, because she's so attuned to her inner processes—in this poem to what she calls "Pain's Successor," to the least dramatic, but for her the most auspicious, aspect of suffering "When the Soul/ Has suffered all it can —" Most of us are so grateful for the relief of pain that we don't notice how in its aftermath it fades into dull depression; in my case, after winter's pain comes the drudgery of mud season and the excruciating waiting: now that the waiting's over—Spring's arrived!—I awake from my drowsy dimness. But there's a cloying aspect to my late-April awakenings. I surprise myself, as do most New England cynics this time of year, with my enthusiasm. My house sits in a hollow with a brook running through it. Its sunlit banks are dusted with spring beauties, tiny pink-white flowers first to bloom after the snow melts. One breath away from snow, they'll vanish under the new leafage in a week or two.

For a moment, I pause and ask if that pain-succumbing-to-dullness was real.

I sing at the top of my lungs, wanting to be heard. But mostly, my singing is little more than a murmur under my breath.

I like to imagine Emily Dickinson sang to herself in her back yard (days like this one turn the darkest curmudgeon into a "blooming" romantic). Dickinson's poems are kin to 19th-century shape-note hymns and anticipate the internal rhymes and mordant ironies—and the failed romance—of last century's popular torch song.

There's a whiff of Dickinson in Billy Strayhorne's "Lush Life," a jazz-proem to rejected lovers and barfly hermits everywhere:

The girls I knew had sad and sullen gray faces
With distingue traces
That used to be there, you could see where
They'd been washed away
By too many through the day
Twelve o'clock tales.

Like Strayhorne's lyrics, I suspect Dickinson's poems were written to be set to song. Her word-play makes eminent pop-song sense, with its rhythmically interruptive caesuras and breathy chattiness intermingled with lyrical ironic concision. But in her case, only the poet can sing her songs. Her "unheard music is sweeter" for me, because I can only imagine the poet singing her poems to herself as she must have hummed hymns she heard in church. But it isn't a pity we'll never hear her music: I prefer the Parthenon without its original gaudy colors and I like my Dickinson half-dumb.

As I go about my business, I think of Emily Dickinson, who really delighted in burrowing-in—in many poems, she declares herself a hermit; in the following lines she stakes her claim as a part-time renunciate:

> The Winters are so short
> I'm hardly justified
> In sending all the Birds away
> And moving into Pod –
>
> Myself—for scarcely settled
> The Phoebes have begun –
> And then—it's time to strike my Tent
> And open House again

It's interesting that she presents us with the phoebe here, a domestic country bird who nests under roof eaves—I call them "dirty birds" as they return to the same spot in our house and don't clean their nests from year to year. The mildly irritated tone of these stanzas belies the speaker's impatience with having to share a too brief solitude with anyone: the "Tent" she's forced to "strike"—the "Pod" of her own solitude—seems fragile and temporary; yet like Noah, she implies she's responsible for not just the returning birds, but for those cattle who starved in winter, though no one, she suggests, "credits" her efforts, however fruitless— or successful—they've been.

Dickinson goes on in the last two stanzas of poem #403 to regret the busy-ness of Spring; the casual breeziness of the first part of her poem doesn't ready us for her final harsh vision, nor does it anticipate a sudden shift in diction preparing us for an allusion to an Old Testament patriarch:

My Summer—is despoiled –
Because there was a Winter—once –
And all the Cattle—starved –

And so there was a Deluge –
And swept the World away –
But Ararat's a Legend—now –
And no one credits Noah –

On looking at the two parts of the poem I've presented separately here, I see clearly how the first stanzas were written independently from the second two. In fact, there's a dramatic cleavage between sections: they might stand alone as individual poems. At a quick glance, there's an incongruity, a missing segue, between the coupled verse paragraphs; but one notices that the poem's form follows its function. As Dickinson observes, "It's mostly interruptions," she's "scarcely settled" before she must adjust to another seemingly disjunct transition.

In so many of her poems, Dickinson wants to subvert our expectations for consonance and harmony. Her slant rhymes ("interruptions"/"once," "away"/"Noah"), her jump-cut transitions, her reluctance to settle matters neatly, mirror a restless temperament struggling to yoke disparate states of mind into coherence: in both poems I've quoted

here, there's no reconciliation—although there's res-
olution—between what the speaker desires and what
is: the patient expires before the Surgeon whose "skill
is late" can minister to him; the hyper-activity of
Spring intervenes before the speaker in #396—whose
"Summer—is despoiled"—may reconcile herself to
the misfortunes of Winter.

↜

It's all unruly out there: the chickens began setting
early, too—normally nothing hatches until at least
June, but we had bantams competing for a klatch, and
finally the hatch with three broody hens scrambling
(no pun intended) to sit on the remaining eggs. We
came home late one night, and forgetting to close
up the hen house proved a near disaster as a coon (I
suspect a coon) stole away with two of our banties.
So we feel like Emily's Noah—but barely afloat (chase
the geese out of the kitchen garden, ward off phan-
tom coons, protect the tender seedlings), and it's all
energetic foolhardiness—the early-blooming flowers
are more than a little silly to have made a show so
prematurely: that stealthy frost will be-head a single
oriental poppy.

We even had our drought early—a thunderous
thaw in early April followed by an April and May of
June weather, the frogs carousing early, thousands of
basso-profundos and screeching peepers. But in early
June the weather did an about-face into a late-winter
issued in by thunderstorms and a tornado warning: it

poured continuously all night, and now the stream's in a heedless burble—and I've discovered our little pond stocked with trout is almost empty, the culprit a heron last fall who looked so picturesque studying its own reflection in the water.

Some of our neighbors are back, but in lesser numbers. Used to be you could hear the answering back and forth of thrushes, especially in the early spring—but this year the xylophonic vireos nearly squelch a single, deep-woods thrush-song. The same with Spring warblers: they return in lesser numbers from Costa Rica, where Starbuck's plantations hurry the demise of our songbirds' Winter habitat. One rule of thumb is not to plant anything but peas and radishes until after the full moon in June; but this year even my wife, a prudent gardener, abandoned caution and put in tomatoes and cucumbers in early May, and planted a few sacrificial tobacco plants; like Thoreau, she seeded a third more beans than we need, for the deer and woodchucks: before the splendid clear nights of the last frost, we wet the garden with a hose to ward off a hard freeze; when this doesn't work, we read Emily Dickinson—a fellow gardener.

When I visited Dickinson's house in Amherst this Spring, I was struck by her flower gardens, kept much the same as she left them, and I tried to imagine her hands scratched and dirty, her white nun's garments damp with sweat. Beneath Dickinson's sense of loss,

there's an acceptance of things as they are, a drawing
in of resources—and I can't help feel her "philosophical attitude" was nurtured by observing the flux and
finality of her own gardens; but though I'd like to find
in her acceptance of tragedy a sunny ambiguity, I'm
left more depressed than breathless, especially in those
poems about frost and flowers, a subject about which
she had intimate knowledge.

What strikes me about her most arresting poems
is how that apparent intimacy overlies a respect for
natural processes; her love of paradox turns a frost into
a windfall, as in Poem 391:

A Visitor in Marl –
Who influences Flowers –
Till they are orderly as Busts –
And Elegant—as Glass –

Who Visits in the Night –
And just before the Sun –
Concludes his glistening interview –
Caresses and is gone –

But who his fingers touched –
And where his feet have run –
And whatsoever Mouth he kissed –
Is as it had not been –

After reading the poem a few times, I recalled view-
ing a collection of glass flowers at Harvard's Peabody
Museum—a collection that opened, actually, in 1886,

the year of Dickinson's death: even if she hadn't seen the Peabody exhibit (she visited Boston only once, to consult an eye doctor), she would have been exposed to the art of glass-flower arrangement (the Victorian rage), and from this might have been tempted to work a glass-flower conceit into her poem.

Dickinson herself made dried flowers collages and gathered them in scrapbooks. I saw examples of her collection at her home; flattened, colorless, they resemble in their desiccation the spare, irregular shapeliness of her poetry, which she gathered in sheaves bound together with thread. I was also reminded of Dickinson's collecting when reading the last stanza of her poem that refers to the alteration of those flowers by "A Visitor in Marl," whose kiss preserves as it destroys.

A fatal kiss, a collector's kiss—or a fleeting lover's midnight kiss.

And I admired how Dickinson balances the frost as a kind of cruel suitor who "Caresses and is gone" against the frost's persona as sculptor "influenc(ing) Flowers—/ Till they are orderly as Busts—/And Elegant—as Glass—"

Dickinson's language also matches the icy elegance of her landscape: while the erotic "s" sounds—those seductive sybillants—hurry the poem along, their twined braidedness contrasts to the freezing of flowers into marbled glass—an event as unexpected as the poem's slant and off-rhymes— "touched"/"kissed," "Sun"/gone"—that replace the expected resonance of true rhyme for something more pliant—and natural.

Dickinson's world in miniature is arresting because of its focused intensity and its fragmented boldness: friends I made while teaching in China were especially fond of her, maybe because translations of her work emphasized the ideographic starkness of the poems; maybe, too, living in a regimented, highly socialized world, they appreciated her love of solitude, a solitude not unlike that of classical China's poets; but mostly it was Dickinson's honest, hard-nosed view of things that proved a tonic in a place where dissimulation is a way of life.

It's easy here, too—in northern New England—to lie to ourselves, to dissimulate. We tell ourselves there's a just plan to the vagaries of nature, when it's evident sometimes that nature bends to us rather than the other way round; our apocalypse is home-grown, man-made.

I also press at the margins: planting too early, I ask too much or I want consistency, when nature is fond of a bedeviling Dickinsonian paradox.

Drunk in the Woods

‿◠

MY AA FRIEND JON Z. and I go out together for the bird count in spring and fall and talk about the years we spent drinking. Jon, who introduced me to bird watching after we both got out of rehab, tells me that, in particle physics, when a particle is observed it becomes a wave—and that Einstein physics also suggests the behavior of phenomena is dependent on the position of their viewer. Does particle physics take into account the attitude of the viewer—are the waves more wavy when I'm seeing them hung over, and, if so, what does this say about how light waves once fell into my whisky-spiked coffee? When he and I go bird watching, we turn back the clock. We look at the world like we saw it drunk and now see it sober. Jon, who's got more experience in this sobriety business, says it's crazy to believe the trees are anything but trees. He says the voices I heard years ago weren't a hallucination, though they would be if I kept hearing them. You hear them once, he says, they're a mystical experience; twice you may be onto something, or you've gone crazy.

I come from an alcoholic family—uncle, aunt, grandfather, and God knows who else, dating back to when man first crushed grapes. Actually, both sides of the family drink. My mother's father died of cirrhosis when he was forty; Mom's sister went in and out of AA, finally succumbing to a lethal cocktail of gin and tranquilizers; my father's brother committed suicide—after a bout of heavy drinking—at the age of twenty-six.

My own drinking landed me in dozens of scrapes. I've been thrown in jail for public drunkenness in three countries, thrown out of bars, got a broken ankle, a fractured skull, a busted jaw in fights I provoked; I've been sued for things I did while drunk, and have lost dozens of friendships.

Fifteen years ago, I'm sitting downstairs in streams of unadulterated early March sunlight sobering up, when I hear the voices coming in the cabin window, electronic voices singing an eerily electronic hallelujah. The "experience" lasts less than a minute, but it's protracted in the snowy light and silence. Five in the morning, late March, a few weeks after town-meeting, and I haven't drunk for three or four days, but this last binge has been so hard things still are reverberating. I would like to say it's my last drunk, but there's almost eight years of them to come: living in a one-room cabin with no electricity or running water is difficult, especially if you're hungover and have to deal with the occasional hallucination. I lean over the cook stove. Newspaper and tinder, a match struck, the sudden flare in the wood box, a burst of flame. And then a little light in the branches, a rustle upstairs in the loft where my wife finally drifts off to sleep.

I'd been leafing through a Bible a few minutes before—my eye kept drifting to the word DOOM that seemed to blast out from every line—when the voices crowded in on me. I immediately think they're angels, an "angelic chorus," something sinister and unearthly, a sort of doomsday chorus, and when they stop, the sound cuts off, like a switch, now you hear them, now you don't. A rocking chair rocks in the amber window light.

The Bible pages flick in an invisible wind.

Hallucination?

I wait to hear them again—half-wanting for them to disappear. And they do. And in a way, they don't.

I sit long in the after-shock, and I'd like to say the experience is accompanied by a moment of clarity, but I'm left feeling empty, confused. I'd expected this to be accompanied by shafts of rapture, or at least pleasure, the hint of exquisite pleasure. I have no idea what the voices were singing. And was it singing, that one sustained *ahh*, that long extended syllable, that crushing inrush of ecstatic air?

I don't tell my wife when she gets up and dresses for work about the voices. And I don't take a drink.

I've forgiven the geese. I've got to forgive the geese.

⌒

Late-winter—a time to hold on or give out. March and April, the suicide months in Vermont. Town Meeting, when I began that drunk those many years ago, was filled with grumpy folks with grudges. I sat with my wife at the back of the Grange Hall counting the number of people I knew from the village, a good portion who drink too much. It's easy to call this a town in denial, but it's more complicated. Shame goes deep in God's country—my theory. With little interest in the town, only a vestige of civic responsibility dragged me into the big, drafty, half-empty hall. But still there was some feistiness left in the crowd and old feuds were rekindled.

A few years before, a guy who on Tuesday was cantankerously arguing taxes hired me for a waitering job at a local restaurant. I worked for him six months, till one night he tried to strangle me because of the way I was mixing the salad oil.

On the walk back, my wife and I discovered a deer carcass, half-submerged under the snow. Coyote and bird tracks spanned out around the carnage of sprayed deer hair, bone-fragments, gristle. We walked up the meadow, past the tumbledown farmhouse I'd watched disintegrate over the years. Though its roof's caved in, the front door's threshold is intact; Corinthian-style

florets on either side of the door are paint-chipped,
ravaged. From the little porch, we looked down the
meadow toward the village tucked in the folds of the
Green Mountains. Behind the old house, wooded
hills rise to the site of more crumbling farmsteads:
we heard the faint trembling of the brook following
the edge of the meadow, a sound both reassuring and
troubling as there was still snow in the mountains and
a thaw—not long away—would bring with it Spring
flooding. I pointed out to my wife the deer stand
where sometimes in the summer I'd spend afternoons
with a book. And then, apropos of nothing, when we
got home I pulled out the vodka bottle hidden in the
hall closet and began drinking.

I'm still drinking three days later.

With raspy mind, I drive into town. At the Mobil
pump filling up my truck's tank, it comes to me that
my error has been to think. A chill wind blows across
the highway, ruffling the pennants, and down our
narrow valley, the mountains butt up against gray sky,
all this fermenting and festering with the indecision
of Spring. So I spend an indecisive five minutes contemplating the ales, the lagers, the wine-coolers; and
I reach inside to touch the cool, sweating neck of a
bottle, an impulse I swat down when I see my wife's
gray Nova drive by—rather, the ghost of a Nova
rounding the bend, its driver, I imagine, terrified at
what she'll find at home.

Such is the nature of my disease, that instead of
heeding my well-intentioned inner voices, I reach in

again, clasp the bottle, unscrew the cap and drink it down. Such is the nature of the town I live in that the checkout girl doesn't even blink when I set the drained bottle on the counter along with a case of Old Milwaukee.

My wife's home for lunch, and we're arguing in the yard. I'm no longer drinking and finally, after days of silence, we're arguing, little disastrous, accusatory balloons writhing out of our mouths. A few days later, a week after I've stopped drinking, I feel blurry and only half-awake, and suddenly she's surprisingly comforting. Or maybe just fed up and waiting out my drying-out period, distrustful, distant, so mistrustful that her guard's frozen into a semi-permanent feint.

Sometimes, I tell Jon, I think there's such a thing as an alcoholic landscape—a drunk landscape, as opposed to the sober one I live in now, the same trees, eight years later, the same brook, but with more clarity, a drunk landscape—apocalyptic late-September apples, a death-rattle waterfall. When I mention my concept of a drunk landscape, he immediately thinks of how the drunk poet Li Po drowned when he reached into the water to grab the moon's reflection. I'm also thinking of a landscape devoid of mystical suggestion which, paradoxically, is rife with symbols and signifiers, and yet, dull and witless, it resists all our attempts at transcendence. A "languagey" landscape, noisy beyond words, that becomes more inaccessible with every drink one takes: it can't be juxtaposed to a sober one full of mystery and nuance; a landscape fully without resonance: there's no echo here, no sweet association, no gentle rush, a bitingly cold morning landscape seen through an icy window so full of dread it can't bring forth the sense of wonder that same frosted-window view provokes for me sober.

The whole week before my first drink had been a time of dying animals: two dead chickens, the carcasses of deer on the ridge above our house. I found one chicken mangled in the coop by the geese who managed to get in during the day: I suspect it was June, the gosling, since she hates chickens, and I'm filled with "justifiable anger" at her though, I know it was my own fault for giving her access to the coop.

The snow continues to fall, a warm, late-winter snow.

Another of our hens died yesterday, a Rhode Island Red—I think it was old age, but I've no idea how old she is. Suzanne saw her out on our porch where we kept her after she got sick. A brief nervous flutter, then Rita was dead. The other dead chicken was the one who sat on eggs. Do the others miss her? Do chickens grieve?

The snow's changed to rain. The geese go out onto the pond and splash around in melted ice-puddles. (Geese sure know how to celebrate.) Real teases, they pretend not to know me when, hungover and shaky, I try to bring them into their shed. My wife and I like to sit on a bale of hay after we've coaxed them in—they like soft, gentle voices which I find difficult to reconcile with the fact they've killed my favorite chicken.

Today, the "voices" are stilled enough for me to throw a line in the brook and catch a little trout that I fry only a few minutes later on the cook stove. I like the first-of-the-season feel of catching the half-limp brookie, but with the water not much above freezing, the fish are only half-awake and in a winter torpor.

I wash out my plate with the hand pump, and I smoke outside in the yard. The snow's gone, the rain's stopped, exposing winter rubbish—broken-off branches, wood ashes, a soggy lost mitten. Water rills down the hollow, a lost echo in the woodsy silence; my hangover magnifies the sound, and, dry-mouthed, I sit down on a stump listening to nothing in particular: there's lots of picking up to do, but most of the stuff's half-frozen to the ground. I manage a few wheelbarrows-full of slushy leaves and cart them to my little dump at the edge of the yard; I look down at the brook, curls of ice clinging to the rocks, and I think of the past week—today's sudden snow, a thaw following what just might be my last drunk: there's lots to consider under the fresh impact of hangover, but it will take years (I don't realize this now) before things sort out.

When I'm sober, I won't regret leaving these moments behind. But what I see is only half the picture; even the few early spring birds—an errant robin, red poles who've been here all winter—are chirpily articulate: the feeder rattles, the hemlocks buzz with haggling chickadees. There's, too, the odd sense that this clarity's a charade, the dress-up of early spring a kind of dumb-show. But then there's the sheer reality, the beauty—and I use that word, "beauty," advisedly: late or early, spring's holding forth in its chilly way. Truth is, it's not spring, yet not wholly not-spring either, but a kind of reluctantly arriving Winter, who, like a late guest (a little petulant and very late in her drab muddy gown), I ignore. Beyond the willows, the slushy deer runs, the frozen sloughs turning to water; but nothing's resolved, it's not over; seeds are scattered, the chickadees and siskins, the yellow-breasted vireos, are on time, punctual, but it's late for them too: the yard's in shadow, the shadows cool and blue, the trees lost in slumber, the day carrying on in sunlight: sliding away in sunlight, the chickens clucking the way only chickens do. The geese easy in their waddle. The pitchfork handle barnacled, sticky with lime. All these in the slow oozings, the rapid thunder-clutter of wings of newer birds gathering in the trees, *cheet-cheet*, then a blurr of feathers, the bobbing whitetail, the quick flit of it, and she's gone, her tracks gone, just as the geese approach, warily at first, around the first tufts of grass, but late, late, the drizzling sleet, and—still winter—the four geese trumpeting down the snowy yard.

For a moment the sun peers out from shifting clouds; needles of light stab the half-frozen surface of the pond. I walk a way down the road, testing my energy. Used to be I'd hide some beer in a culvert, but today I have no stash. The bank beside the road is awash with runoff. Rivulets from the hillside crease where last year's rye grass hasn't taken. More water than usual has come down the mountain since a logger did some harvesting last spring, and skidder ruts stand out against the muddy ground; a litter of slash from downed spruce, stumps of once-towering tamarack, testify to the logger's carnage: if I knew better, I'd see some lesson in this, but nothing impacts, it's all just stuff, echoes in the brainpan.

In a few years after I get sober, much of this will look and taste differently. But it's all stuff and junk. Usually it takes at least a month not drinking until things start to register. Despite those years when I didn't drink, I've never known a clarity that comes by setting things right with the world. There's talk of synergy between the mind and nature, but I only have it when I'm high. If I were drunk or just sobering up, all this would be inert, expendable, framed by a gilded, twenty-four caret hangover.

⌒

Now the cabin's actually a house, with a modest addition of a bathroom and two bedrooms, a deck looking out to the pond; the outhouse we used for eight winters is tilted on its side, and the road that was once so bad we had to walk it most times of the year is navigable, and we even plow it in winter. We still keep chickens, a few geese; there's brook trout in the pond, a kitchen garden and a larger "industrial garden." Lunch today—three big trout and sunny-side-up eggs, boiled potatoes with fresh chives, sliced garden tomatoes. The trout bellies are an autumn gold. Sunlight falls across the deck onto my wife's tanned arms. Henry, our beautiful rooster, struts across the grass—those bold black hearts on his white chest imperial against the late summer green.

My wife and I rarely talk about my drinking, but beneath our serenity, there's a tacit understanding that all this is provisional: the farther away I am from drinking, the closer I am to another drink: that's the paradox, says Phil, another AA friend, whose own mystical experience in the woods came to him years ago when he worked as a logger up in the Cold Hollow Mountains for Atlas Plywood; of course he was drunk. Each day he'd drink a case of beer on his skidder miles from the road, and if he'd chain-sawed his leg, there'd have been no one to rescue him. This happened around the time he was hitting bottom. His drinking would begin before he went out in the morning, and so he was shaky, and he'd begun to fear that someday he might not get back home in the evening, and if he didn't return, it might not matter to anyone. So he's winched his come-along thirty feet up the big white pine. He's tied it to his skidder, and he's sawing through the pine when a squirrel scurries down and chatters to my friend about how the pine is his home, generations of squirrel ancestors have lived here, and he should be ashamed, not only because he's destroying squirrel habitat, but destroying himself. He swears he walked out of the woods that day, leaving the skidder and chainsaw, the pine he'd begun cutting, its family of squirrels unmolested, and that his moment of truth in the mountains was the start of his sobriety.

His story would be less credible were he not such an empirical guy or if I didn't know a few other liquored-up loggers like he was—like I was—careening around with real or metaphorical chainsaws: this stoned, drunk border landscape goes on being itself, goes on permutating not only with the seasons, but with changes in synapses and blood chemistry.

A drunk landscape, as I recall it, busy attending to itself, unwilling to give out secrets: I remember waking up in it one July afternoon after falling asleep while drinking in the woods. I hadn't walked far from the house, and had sat down under some hemlocks to finish my beer: I'd been drinking all morning and had reached the point where things oscillate from awful to splendid in a matter of moments, and before I fell asleep, I experienced that false ecstasy that comes less and less frequently to long-time drunks: the hemlock needles wavered, the sound of the brook rose weakly from below, where I could see the little white plumes of a waterfall, and I recalled, just before I'd fallen asleep, my wife standing in the garden where, years later, I'd lay stones for a patio: she was slender and small next to the lawn, beautiful and tragic.

And when I awoke, there were no images, I had little to cling to but an abstract neediness.

A drunk landscape lays down harsh rules, those "thou shalt nots" that come from a stormy Old Testament God of the Burning Bush, of Flaming Tablets: it's opaque, brittle, unlike the supple transparency of a landscape seen sober. I experience the permeability of a sober landscape when I glide in my canoe through the reeds on the edge of a pond, or when I resist an urge to get up from my hammock and attend to my responsibilities.

I'm flattering myself. I 'd like to say I feel like a Zen Dagwood, taking a T'aoist snooze, funny papers strewn across my lap (fact is I have a Blondie of a wife with a list of chores I need to attend to). I admit that these observations derive partly from self-admonishments against projecting onto the world my own drunk scenarios. I won't say a sober landscape is non-utilitarian, though that's partly what it's about. There's simply nothing to be got from it, as it serves no God-given purpose other than to be itself; no miracles are performed, no transformations take place. No great problems are solved. No secrets are revealed.

A drunk in a drunk landscape wants sweeping views, breathtaking vistas; he wants the landscape of yesterday or tomorrow; wants the basket of fresh tomatoes and summer squash to be stamped with the *Good Housekeeping* seal; he wants the night to be moonlit and long.

Ugly Beauty

"The number of humble-bees in any district depends in a great degree on the number of field-mice, which destroy their combs and nests; and Mr. H. Newman, who has long attended to the habits of humble-bees, believes that 'more than two-thirds of them are thus destroyed all over England.' Now the number of mice is largely dependent, as every one knows, on the number of cats; and Mr. Newman says, 'Near villages and small towns I have found the nests of humble-bees more numerous than elsewhere, which I attribute to the number of cats that destroy the mice.' Hence it is quite credible that the presence of a feline animal in large numbers in a district might determine, through the intervention first of mice and then of bees, the frequency of certain flowers in that district!" —Charles Darwin

Humble Bees

Though there's been a honey bee drought across the States and across the world in the last few years, we have no lack of "humble" bees (otherwise known as 'bumble bees"). In fact, as our cat population increases (we have five of them), so do the bumble bees. I don't

know if cats protect the honey bees from mice—
bumble bees nesting underground are vulnerable to
mice, while honey bees nest well above ground and
have different predators. Over the past thirty years,
three generations of cats have adopted us. Our first
lived to the age of twenty-two. Our second beloved, a
six-toed coon cat, succumbed early to feline leukemia
just after we moved into our cabin. Three cats have
been eaten by coyotes and fisher cats. Our current
five cats are orphans: Bianca, a starvation-thin white
female, arrived on our doorstep as a kitten; Brigitte,
a plump calico, faring better here than with a mostly
absent neighbor, came to us while young. We were
bequeathed Annie, a runty tortoise with a mouse-like
tail, by my sister on her deathbed in 2004. Before
her rescue, Annie had been living in my sister's upper
west-side NY apartment, subsisting on roaches and
toilet water for six weeks. There's also Pucho, a
panther-black male, and Laurie (named improbably
after my college roommate), a twenty-pound male
tiger. All five cats catch and eat bugs and mice and an
occasional chickadee (we no longer keep bird feeders,
which lessens bird-death). We keep them in after sunset, and don't let them out till mid-morning.

I'm sure Charles Darwin was a cat lover. I imagine him in his English garden, where he gathered
specimens for his first botanical experiments, contemplating a "humble bee" half-drowned in nectar
whose bumbling sounds not unlike a cat's purr
(when I was a kid, I impressed people by catching

bumble bees in a jar; I'd tame them and make bumblebee necklaces and bracelets for my friends). A fat tabby in Darwin's lap, his milky blue eyes reflecting the agate English sky.

W. H. Kirchnen and J. Röschard, two Swiss bee experts, tell us that, "Bumblebees (*Bombus terrestris*) react to disturbances within the nest by a conspicuous hissing sound. The sound is characterized by a high intensity in the ultrasonic frequency range. It is elicited by vibrations of the nest and by mammalian breath and artificial air currents containing CO_2. Domestic mice entering a bumblebee nest elicit these sounds and retreat immediately in response to the bumblebees' signal. It is concluded that the hissing sounds serve as aposematic warning signals aimed at predators entering the nest."

While bumblebees make hissing noises to ward off mice, they make contrastingly soothing bumbles as they besot themselves in our garden. There's always a cat snoozing on the deck while another cat watches the snoozing cat. In the evening, as dusk rises up through the cornflowers, a few nectar-drunk bumblebees sub-audibly hum. Unlike the flitting honeybee, they stumble flower to flower, weighted down by pollen and nectar, in no rush to get home.

Then at the end of a hot summer day, if we haven't already scooted our cats into the house, our calico sashays to the brook where it's cool. After she performs her ablutions and has a nap, she'll be back, a mouse clenched in her jaws, pleased with herself.

Are cats narcissists? Ours seem to know where they look good—sitting sphinx-like beneath a rosehip bush, or atop an embroidered cushion.

⌐

Many years ago, our cat Maggie birthed a litter of defective kittens. All died, save a black-and-white fellow we called "Little Louis." Because of his repeated seizures, we decided to "put him to sleep." We drove him to our veterinarian, a garrulous dude named Simon Wexler—a disciple of the Avatar Meyer Baba, whose photograph grinned at us across the vet's desk (with his handlebar mustache and goofy grin, Baba resembled the comedian-trombonist Jerry Colonna).

While we were in the vet's messy office, Louis seized several times—he was getting worse.

"He's been having these fits all morning," I said. "There's no way he can keep on like this."

"Euthanizing is against my core principals," Simon said.

"The little guy is suffering," Suzanne replied. "God, anybody can see that."

"That may be so," the vet said with a bloodless smile.

"Isn't it your job, really, to prevent suffering?"

"It's also my job to save life, to protect life," he said.

Louis seized a few more times, and we left the vet's office and drove home. His seizures kept on till I drowned him in the brook behind our house. The loveliness of that spot deep in the hemlocks was destroyed by his last moments clenching and unclenching his limbs and clawing against me—and by a migraine that shot jagged yellow auras across my vision. For a few minutes, I went blind. Then, the visual migraine became a brain-splitting headache. Of course, no migraine is simple. Stress and confusion trigger migraines—and my stress came after killing Little Louis.

The Dog Cat

For every saint who's found a way to exit this world in good conscience, millions work off their karma by putting a bullet in the head of a pet or farm animal, and feel like shit in the bargain. I won't argue the merits of drowning Louis, don't know if it's earned me points in heaven or hell, but I carried his body into the woods and buried him, and afterward I sat alongside the pool where he'd drowned: in my story's least credible moment, the Dog Cat emerges like Ra The Egyptian Sun God, who changes himself into a cat to do battle with the serpent-like darkness. He sits on the bank across from me, big as a medium-sized dog. I've never seen him before or since—nor has Suzanne, who glimpsed him just once and vouches for my sanity in the matter—but his after-image stayed with us. His most impressive aspect was his size and a pair of slashed-up cocker spaniel ears—and the timing of his appearance moments after Louis died. He sat there, sizing me up, looking ordinary save that he was neither cat nor dog, but something from a dream I wish I never had.

Maybe he was a descendant of barn cats who've lived around North Country farms for years. There's scores of them in the woods, feral and scrappy, birthing kittens, most which die their first winter. Now that most dairy farms have shut down, they've been forced out to live in abandoned sheds and barns, the fittest begetting even fitter, fiercer progeny, like the one who escorted Louis into another world.

The Dog Cat, the Ur Cat. The biggest fucking cat in the valley.

Of course, I leave open the possibility that this animal was a rare cross, a theoretically impossible cross, between a dog and a cat.

His most singular aspect was a fearsome ugliness.

Thence followed a decade of hard times. We were so poor we couldn't afford to "fix" our cats. We fed them cheap cat food supplemented with trout from our brook. Around this time our six-toed cat Cedric, a mythical fellow himself, returned, skinny and sick, after being gone for several months. Who knows why he disappeared or why he came back. Being he was an unfixed tom I suspect had a lot to do with it. Within three months, Cedric was dead of feline leukemia. We had one cat left, Maggie, a midget-sized mouser, Louis's mother.

We finally fixed Maggie—she lived another fifteen years hunting our woods all day and curled up at night on our hearth.

HOMONCULUS

During those down-and-out times, I had a series of troubling dreams.

In one, I'm sitting at the same spot where I drowned Louis on Dreamer's Brook. I cast my fishing line into the shallow water and come up with a little silver man tangled and struggling on my line—he is no larger than my hand. As I reel him in, he turns into a bird flicking its silver wings. I reach out to touch the bird, and it loses its mobility, goes flat and two-dimensional. The moment before the bird changes into a dead image, a piece of gleaming art, still spooks me: the feathers are wet, real bird's feathers, silvery and shiny, and a voice tells me I'm fishing in a sacred spot, that ancient wagons have rolled by here, children have fished here, and a kitten drowned here.

What strikes me about my dream is how it metamorphosed through a complex of emotional imperatives into a little man, then into a bird. My desire to control my mental projection was embodied in the string that snared in the little man's limbs. In turn, the man was liberated into the form of a silver bird—a bird that was changed into art, after which it vanished.

I report the dream with some embarrassment. I'm not especially superstitious, but as dreams go (apologies for this one), it was instructive, if not transforming, for me during that time.

UGLY BEAUTY

In the New York Botanical Garden's Haupt Conservatory, which I recently visited, arcing shafts of hollyhock, delphinium, and larkspur embrace a partial replica of Darwin's study at Down House. You arrive at the study on a facsimile of the "sandwalk," well known to Darwin scholars, on which the naturalist mused over questions posed by the curve of a stem or a flower's distinctive form. It's a lovely place, a kind of doll house for botanists, removed from the city's hubbub. One looks out Darwin's study window at a rectangle of bare earth intended to replicate an experimental plot, his "weed garden," where he tested his ideas on natural selection. Here, and in the meadows, bog, and orchard surrounding Down House, Darwin's estate in Kent, England, he observed cross-pollination (till then, more a concept than a reality among Darwin's scientist-contemporaries) in his "weed garden." During the summer of 1857, obsessed with the process of sexual and a-sexual reproduction as he witnessed it in the primroses, orchids, and carnivorous plants in his garden, he wrote: "There is grandeur in this view of life, with its several powers, having been originally breathed into a few forms or into one; and that, whilst this planet has gone cycling on according to the fixed law of gravity, from so simple a beginning endless forms most beautiful and most wonderful have been, and are being, evolved."

Darwin's obsession, which had carried him 'round the Horn to the Galapagos as the H.M.S. Beagle's botanist, was still operative years later, back home. Intrigued with a carnivorous pitcher plant so small it could be held in a man's palm, he fed it egg white, cinders, bits of wood, even chloroform, attempting to understand why and how it had developed its ability to feed upon insects, and what caused it to close its sticky trap. By the end of that summer, he figured out the anatomy of all local orchid species, and was able to show not only that cross-fertilization happened, but that it predicted what the pollinator for each variety would look like, based on the flower shape.

He also wrestled with the idea of the utility of beauty—its usefulness. In *The Origin of the Species* he wrote:

> I willingly admit, that a great number of male animals, as all our gorgeous birds, some fishes, reptiles and mammals, and a host of magnificently coloured butterflies have been rendered beautiful for beauty's sake; but this has been effected through natural selection, that is by the more beautiful males having been continually preferred by the females, and not for the delight of man. So it is with the music of birds. We may infer from all this that a nearly similar taste for beautiful colors and for musical sounds runs through a large part of the animal kingdom. When the female is as beautifully coloured as the male, which is not rarely the case with birds and butter-flies, the cause apparently lies in the colours acquired by sexual selection having been transmitted to both sexes, instead of to males alone. How the sense of beauty in its simplest form—that is, the reception

of a peculiar kind of pleasure from certain colours, forms, and sounds—was first developed in the mind of man and in the lower animals, is a very obscure subject. The same sort of difficulty is presented, if we enquire how it is that certain flavors and odours give pleasure, and others displeasure. Habit in all these cases appears to have come to a certain extent into play; but there must be some fundamental cause in the constitution of the nervous system in each species.

～

In his discussion of beauty's role in natural selection, Darwin didn't reconcile the utility of beauty's dark twin—ugliness. We acknowledge our own attraction in fairy tales and opera to ugliness; in these stories, for every Beauty there's a Beast, for every swan there's an ugly duckling. But it's not just ugliness that attracts us. We are drawn to the vulnerable and the doomed in ways that go beyond Darwin's theory. In fairy tales, we're rewarded for perceiving nobility and/or beauty beyond the façade of ugliness. In nature, and in our stories and myths, females are attracted to brutishly ugly males, who become their protectors. But rarely in real life do we find animals attracted to and protective of the weak, even of their own species. Mating doesn't have to do with connecting up with the lame and the halt—it's only humans whose compassion can be translated into desire.

We might call that desire altruistic, but I suspect, as Darwin says, there is some fundamental cause in the constitution of the nervous system in (our) species at work in our attraction to the misshapen and the ill-born. It may be a genetically driven desire to get some diversity—some ugly beauty—into the gene pool. Or we may sense an advantage in bonding or coupling with a creature who has no endearing physical characteristics, but whose sensitivities, because of the challenges their ugly ancestors met in life and have handed down to them, are heightened.

Darwin in His Garden

My experience with and my feelings toward Louis are common. Granted, there are ways I might put my compassion to better use than to write about the death of a kitten. But imagination, not compassion or the lack thereof, is the culprit today: I imagine Darwin in his Kent garden, pausing among the larkspur. Nine o'clock in the evening and the sun hangs like a pewter bowl on the horizon. A few humble bees grope in the still-open foxglove. Darwin lights a cigar. Having drunk more than his share of Armagnac, he remembers a day out from Port Stanley in the Falkland Islands five years ago seeing the vast King Penguin rookeries. Due southwest, in the Straits of Magellan three weeks away, he'd watch an albatross astride the looming waves and hear the first mate's cry, and high in the rigging, the singing stays. And all that white space, that aimless nothing.

And he would have relit his cigar and stared into the darkness of his garden.

III

WINDFALL

⌒

I STUMBLE OUT OF THE RAIN into the grim little office at Maple Leaf Farm in the town of Underhill and sign the insurance and registration forms. On the bedside table between my roommate and me lies Alcoholics Anonymous, the AA bible. I don't skim more than a few lines before there's a clap of thunder. I look out through the café curtains past the Maple Leaf van to a group of smokers under the cafeteria eaves, most of them guys in their early thirties.

"This your first time in here?" my roommate asks. "Not me. I know this place like the b-back of my h–h–hand." But the back of his hand is trembling. And I'm still high. Unshaven, in dirty jeans and mud-caked boots, there's nothing about me that says I'm not an alcoholic. My roommate has a trimmed military mustache, pressed chinos and a sleeveless muscle-shirt. You wouldn't notice him on the street, wouldn't have seen him in the line at Walmart, the pudgy long-haired guy dressed in chinos and a muscle shirt, puking his eyes out in front of me. It goes without saying that when our dinner finally arrives, I touch none of it. Just before dark, roomie and I attend our first AA meeting; then we go on the porch to a splintery picnic table and our counselor-social worker, Kate, plump, fifty-ish, and red-headed, sets out some water colors and asks us to paint an image of our drinking lives. Tim paints a purple-and-black "Cookie Monster," all hairy with sad, bulged-out eyes and a red Santa Claus nose. But I'm image-less. Tim's painted in lurid sprawly reds and blacks the story of his childhood—a stick-figure child wanders frightened and amazed through a junkyard of beer bottles and crashed cars. But I'm running on empty, and suddenly, flames lick and leap onto the paper. I'm standing in a burning house, completely naked, a self-immolating alcoholic crazy man.

"That's really f-fucked up," roomie says, glancing at my artwork. Meanwhile, he's pouring out scene after scene from his drinking past.

"What does that make you feel?" the social worker asks him.

"It makes me feel p-pissed off."

"How pissed off? What kind of pissed off?"

"None of your goddamn business," he says.

Next morning, it's raining hard. The little brook behind Maple Leaf has over-run its banks, and the driveway is slathered with mud. I shower and shave and plot my escape: I'll go out for a smoke, hit the road and hitch back to where there's still a part of that quart of gin. But instead, Tim and I shuffle off to the main hall and the day's first "step meeting." None of us here has more than two weeks' sobriety, and the room crackles with low-level delirium. The subject of the first step is "powerlessness": "We realized we were powerless over alcohol," that we couldn't stop drinking, not without getting abjectly down on our knees.

The utter banality of this proposition makes me feel even sicker.

As we settle into our chairs, I'm praying, make me whole again. I'm praying for Tim, too, who's had a bad time of it since he painted his autobiography, which is where the chairperson of the meeting comes in, a girl of around twenty-five, pretty enough to keep all the male eyes—and most of us are male—glued on her. The softness in her voice (hi, I'm Helen, and I'm an alcoholic) tells you she's long since graduated rehab. After the formalities—the Serenity Prayer, a reading of the Steps—Helen "briefly qualifies" with her own story. Her father was a Hollywood stunt man who in the late '80s fled with his family to Vermont and died after a heroin overdose, leaving Helen and her mom penniless. Helen's mom began to drink and died herself in a few years, from liver disease; Helen drank through junior and senior high, and by eleventh grade was an unwed teenage mother with a fetal alcohol syndrome baby. She hit bottom one below-zero night, when police found her passed out in the snow in a Burlington park. I can't keep my eyes off Helen, who's risen from alky angel to rehab Madonna (not that she's turned the place into a revival tent). A few guys doze off in the back while others count the minutes till their next smoke. But there's an attentive group of listeners, of which Tim and I are a part. "This is my third time in here," he says. "I'm triple-retreaded." A sad sigh goes through the room as he tells us about his last lost weekend, ending in a small-town jail where a kindly old AA guy coaxed him through the shakes and drove him through the rain next morning to Maple Leaf.

We stand outside in the rain after the meeting, alkies under a pine tree, druggies beneath a leaf-turning maple, and there's wood smoke in the air, the wet mulch smell of early autumn. Tim's not his usual self—not that I know what that is, but this isn't it. Having offered up his story after Helen qualified, he wants to talk more, but he can't finish a sentence without stuttering into apologies. Having been through rehab before, he's scared silly that, when he gets out, he'll "pick up" again. It's the moment of choice when he's peppered by rationalizations that lead nowhere but to a nearby bar that frightens him.

"I guess nothing's to be done about it." He laughs and rubs his regretful nose.

It's raining even harder now and the others have

gone in, leaving us in the parking lot by the roaring brook behind the detox building. "What I got to do is think about the things I enjoy, like hiking; those th-th-things I used to love to do."

"Hiking?"

"Yeah, hiking," he says. "Been into the woods and mountains all my f-f-fucking life."

I wander off and return to my room to spend the half-hour before our next meeting in mindless, mental hair-splitting. What is it about this "program" that makes me angry? After some cogitation, I attribute it to the fear—like Tim's—that I'll die drunk, that I'll have this needy drunk's personality till I die. Unlike lucky Helen, who lived and found AA, I might not get a second chance, and if I live, I might end up half-sober, needy like now, expiring eventually of some alcoholic disease and blaming everybody but myself. But I'm more at home here among the discards and retreads than anywhere else.

"At least the wheels are turning," Tim says, after I share my thoughts. He's come to fetch me for the next meeting on the porch of Maple Leaf's main building, where the others sit around with their coffee and cigarettes, talking about ACCEPTANCE. A dark, skinny, mid-thirty-ish woman tells how she was given a leave-of-absence from her job at a local junior high after she chased a student around the gymnasium with a hockey stick. "I didn't know how God-loving helpless I was till the kids dragged me kicking and screaming to the principal's office. Problem now," she says, "is I'm thinking too much. Am I supposed to think or not think?"

Helen says sagely that it's not a matter of thinking, but how one thinks. One should avoid "stinking thinking." But which is it we're supposed to do? AA urges us drunks to make bold moves to change our lives, while cautioning restraint and forbearance. These contradictions are hard to wrap my mind around, and the idea that I'll have to live with them all my life keeps me from going into this with an accepting heart.

I've spent most of my life analyzing things, and for what? I'm curious about things spiritual and have known moments of boundless contemplation, but deep thought is nothing without meaningful action. I've dithered in the introspective backwaters, avoided the crowd with nothing to come of it; gone to meditation retreats—but I'm still empty.

I mope around till lunch, fighting off the screaming meanies

Now it's twelve-thirty, just after lunch, and I feel better. Actually, I feel terrific. I'm on a pink cloud of AA LOVE, and see myself as an insignificant piece of shit and as a recovering success story. How long will these mood-swings last? I take a catnap in a porch recliner and dream I'm in a bar where everyone's speaking a foreign language. The bartender offers me a frothy mug of beer, and before I bring it to my lips, Tim shakes me awake.

I follow him into the common room where an old, robust-looking guy, one of the Maple Leaf grounds crew, takes the podium. His story starts in New Jersey with a hair-raising tale of driving the wrong way on the Garden State. "I was flyin'," he says. "Oncoming cars dodging me, troopers chasing me in the opposite lane. You know how that highway dips and curves, the prettiest highway in Jersey, that's where I am at four in the morning with my blood-alcohol three times the limit. I come out of my blackout as I swerve to avoid oncoming traffic and end up in the center island. I stumble out of the car and don't know where the fuck I am. I'm booked and thrown in a drunk tank, all the while insisting on a lawyer, I need a goddamn lawyer! I am this important person, a bank executive! So gimme a lawyer." He mops his brow, looks out at us fellow sufferers. "And that's what my story's all about—pulling strings, wielding influence. Over the years I snuck out of a thousand chances to get sober!" The guy's story is so alive, I have a hard time accepting he hasn't had a drink in thirty years.

Here's another contradiction: to keep the illness at bay, you've got to hang it in all its ugliness where you can see it the rest of your life. At the same time, you need to remind yourself that you've undergone a radical transformation.

Meanwhile, the rain pounds down. Someone had a hard time of it after the last meeting—seizures, convulsions, the works—and the van spirits him or her away with a blatting horn. We're on the porch watching a dim sun exit into the hills west of Mount Mansfield, and the woods are soft and purple, the wind turns up the leaves, exposing their pale under-sides. After dinner, Tim tells me about his job with the Department of Fish and Wildlife. "A glorified game keeper is what I am," he says, and goes on to describe his average day, monitoring the level of beaver dams and slapping mosquitoes while he fights skirmishes with the federal bureaucracy. "It's a good job—too bad I screwed it up so b-b-badly," he says.

⤳

The road from Underhill is washed out, and since the van left, no one can come in or leave. Another dirt road climbs over the Mount Mansfield foothills to Stowe Village: that too is impassable. A backhoe makes its way up the road and plows a dike along the brook. More thunder rolls, lightning flashes, and the lamps blink inside the common room.

A couple of hours before dusk, Tim and I break Maple Leaf rules and walk into the rain-soaked woods behind the farm. The rain stops, a north wind comes up, and the air holds the threat of a damp, cold night. At the top of the hill, there's a weathered old sugar house with rusty sap buckets stacked around. An almost full moon glints through the clouds, and darkness sweeps up from the hollows. We follow a logging road along a stone wall that brings us to the crest of another hill, and the valley's spread before us, the flooding river, the lights of a few towns and some lowly mountains beyond. We stand quiet awhile, and then walk on through more sugar bush; then we're back into the pungent softwoods, and we both know we're lost, inconsequentially lost if not for the fact that we risk suspension from the program for being AWOL.

We try to retrace our steps down into a gully, slogging through acres of sumac and thickets of swamp alders. Tim stutters something about the two of us being crazy, we're crazy as coots, he says. Is madness an innate condition of the alcoholic soul? Is it curable, and how do we know when we're cured? We ascend the gully and rest on another hilltop, but the valley is obscured by the trees, and Tim's talking about the afternoon a few days ago when he drove over Gus, his beloved basset hound. He'd been drinking at Eden Lake with game-warden friends and got in a row with one of them. A few fishermen were out on the lake, trout were jumping at the fly-hatch, and the two wardens were having a grand old time beating the piss out of each other when Tim charged off in his pickup and a half-hour later slammed into his little dog, who stood out in his driveway to greet him. The anticlimactic short-end of this is that Tim and I ford one more mountain stream, hump it past a tumble-down farmhouse, and find ourselves in a cow pasture behind The Farm. At past ten o'clock, people are wandering off to bed. "When an idea comes into my head, I don't let it go," a woman named Ella in a dirty pink jersey mutters to no one in particular. "But I haven't had an idea in the last twenty-four hours." And then a minute or two later she says, "No, that's not true." Four of us stay up past curfew, Tim, me, and two other recovering drunks, cursing the day we were born while the moon lifts into the righteous heavens.

Tim keeps talking long after we head back to our room and I've signed off for the night. He's a talker, I'm a reader, I absorb things better when I read—AA literature in this case— than I do through the spoken word, but my problem is that I concentrate on the messenger rather than the message. It's past midnight. I breeze through a biography of Bill W., co-founder of Alcoholics Anonymous. Not everyone's lucky as Bill W. who had a mystical experience that caused him to stop drinking the last time he was drying out. He sat up in his hospital bed, the room filled with dazzling light, and the craving was lifted from him. Such blessings are rare. Most of us obsess over booze long after we get sober, and not all of us, including Bill Wilson, a depressive all his life, keeps his "serenity."

In his last years, he searched for more God-filled moments. He read William James' *Varieties of Religious Experience*, corresponded with Carl Jung and became friends with Aldous Huxley. Looking for a way out of depression, he experimented with LSD; this did not stop him from crippling guilt and night-terrors. On his death-bed, he cried out for a drink. What does that say about our own progress toward accepting our condition? The thing is, I don't want a drink, not now, maybe never.

I sleep a few hours and wake at six with bed-spins. A fusillade of coughs accompanies my first morning cigarette. Then a rushing shot of vertigo and full-bore adrenaline as I pull on my running shorts and Maple Leaf T-shirt. I take a deep breath, do a couple of manic knee-bends, and say the "Serenity Prayer," then sit cross-legged on the hard cold floor and try to meditate. In my mental condition, a state of total spiritual bankruptcy, I'm incapable of little but weird, semi-hallucinating thoughts.

~

The next half-hour, I pace around the common-room porch waiting for the coffee machine to fire up. There's a pots-and-pans clatter in the kitchen, two stray mutts tousling out on the wet grass, and me stricken by early morning terror as I watch the dawn come up. The Unitarian Church where I first had an inkling of the mystical was on a tree-lined street in a big white house with a wide, sagging porch like this. On summer mornings, Sunday school classes were held on the porch where we watched sailboats tack across Long Island Sound. I liked going to church services more than Sunday school. I sat in back with my little sister as the choir, led by a local opera-singer celebrity, burst into the song "Trees." "I think that I shall never see/ a thing as lovely as a tree," they sang, and then the minister's voice rose in rolling cadences. I loved how the minister mopped his brow and gazed out past the congregation at a willow tree in the courtyard, and I loved the way he pronounced "Gawd" and grimly smiled. Reverend Weary (his real name!) was barely in his forties and gone bald and gray. I liked the elevated way the words drifted from his mouth. While I didn't understand them, they made me feel bigger than myself. Who knows what I got out of Weary's long-winded sermons that posed more questions about God than they answered—but I felt very big-hearted when we left church. Sometimes we'd stop at Louie's Bar on the bay for a late breakfast, and while my father drank his morning cocktail, I wandered the tide flats with my sister and held onto the warm feeling I had in church.

The moment came back to me from time to time—but after I succumbed to alcohol less and less frequently. I have a hard time letting go. At the same time I want to be loved, I crave it. With drink in hand, I crave another drink, and to get it, I represent myself as the most wronged and wretched person on earth. For every rich man, there're a hundred poor ones, and for every million ungenerous souls, someone out there cares about the world. But if you're not helping yourself, you're backsliding; likewise, if you're dreaming of a drink rather than having one, you're not in that much trouble.

That's what Kate, my social worker, tells me at breakfast. "As long as you keep your eye on that drink, keep it in your headlights, you're doing all right."

I follow her out into the sunlight, where we're joined by Tim. The morning clouds have worn off—it's going to be a beautiful day. Kate asks if anyone's up for discussing the BIG BOOK before we drive to an AA meeting in St. Albans, and we sit down on the porch to read AA co-founder Doctor Bob's story of becoming a drunk in a straight-laced Vermont family. Each of us reads a paragraph. Meanwhile, my mind's still going a mile a minute. If I were a less imperfect person, most of my pain would come by reflecting on the suffering I've caused others. But the truth is, all my life I've focused on how I've been done in and who did it to me. Spiritually speaking, I'm bone dry.

At the end of Big Book Discussion, I drift into a first-drink reverie: it's one of those after-church Sundays, and we're again at Louie's. My father's drunk, and my mother has gone back weeping to our station wagon. It's getting toward noon. The fishermen have arrived. The juke box blares out Sinatra, and my father digs into a basketful of juicy clams. I'm there, but I'm not there—Sinatra's singing, my father's grinning, and when the whisky he's made me drink hits my stomach, I reach for another swig just to prove I can do it.

"I can't get that moment out of my head," I tell Kate as we head down to the van with our gang of Maple Leafers. "I can taste the whisky—like I just drank it."

Kate slides into the van's driver seat, takes a swig of her coffee, and shakes her head. I get in next to Tim on one side and Ella on the other. We're on our way to that AA meeting in St. Albans, and I push my baseball cap over my eyes, wary of being out in the world again. Our Lady of Perpetual Snow sits on a hill overlooking the town square. The church annex is thick with cigarette smoke and the muskiness of

AA meetings. But it's a good meeting. Afterwards, Tim and I go into the church: the incense candles flicker, and on the cross above the altar hangs a bleeding wooden Christ, his eyes smoldering red. Once, I believed that we all worship the same God, but here I feel cut off from the warm, accepting religion I grew up in. For starters, I was told that Jesus was a man of reason, and while such men are rare, as a kid I thought we all could be just like he was.

Back at the farm a few hours later I have a dizzy spell. I mope around after dinner, catching pieces of conversation, and what I hear makes little sense—especially my infernal internal monologue. Tim says I'm in denial. "Your mind and body have slipped gears and sent you back to the emotional starting point of your sobriety," he says. "Most of us deny the past, but you're denying your f-f-future." A quick self-diagnosis tells me that I am denying just about everything, and I lean back in the porch recliner and listen to the late-summer rain as Tim carries on. "See those guys over there?" and he points to a new bunch of recruits on the porch of Detox. "That's w-w-what we used to be. Three days makes a difference. You gotta act like it does." I puzzle over Tim's AA philosophy. In a nutshell, it means "Dreaming Makes It True." But I not only deny that I have a drinking problem—I deny the dream that I'm getting better each day I don't drink.

At the evening AA meeting, I can hardly sit still, filled as I am with cold anticipation. Just before twilight, the rain stops. I walk up the road past a field grown over with burdocks. There's a beaver pond down in a hollow and a neglected orchard where a pair of white-tail are munching windfall apples. The sight of me doesn't disturb them, and before the road dives into spruce forest, I see a young girl, no more than eleven or twelve, with albino-white hair leaning on a stone wall, and I'm gravity-less. She appears so suddenly out of nowhere, is so pure an extract of memory (rather than a memory itself), that for a moment I doubt what I see.

⤸

Two days later, on Friday, Tim's AA handshake can't convince me I've made the right choice leaving Maple Leaf early. I slump into our Subaru beside my breezily friendly wife, and when we stop at a convenience store, I'm awash in quandariness. Past the beer and wine cooler I go, and then retrace my steps and regard the bottles with dread. At home I kiss my wife, murmuring that I just don't want to leave, that I belong here, I don't want to go. "But you have to," she says, "that's part of the arrangement."

I'm a real nut-case. I pack a bagful of clothes, bid my wife farewell, and head off in my truck to a buddy's empty cabin on the other side of the mountains.

⤸

I walk in and brush some mouse shit off the table, and then load up the stove to burn off the damp. Peter's off teaching in New Brunswick and has loaned me his place as long as I want. The cabin looks the same: same piano (out of tune), schoolroom chairs, and a loft upstairs with a little window looking on a weedy pond. After dark, I climb up to the loft and sleep comes easy to me. Very early next morning, I walk to a meadow and pick a coffee can of late-season blackberries. I eat the berries, then take the tarpaulin off Peter's canoe and tote it to the landing, and push out into the reeds and open water. Right away, a pair of loons with a little one shows up. The male dives and emerges near my canoe, the female trailing her baby in her wake. The pond, a couple of miles long, is all shallow warm-water with marsh grass, blue-and-green water lilies, and a view of silvery mountains.

Out of the cove and midway across, I look out on a shore lush with paper birch and poplars, my eyes shifting to a rocky cliff where two ravens circle their nest. I see a clump of muddy branches on an overhang, then the scrawny, ugly-headed body of a fledgling raven. Then his squawky, baby raven voice, the sudden flutter of black wings, and he's out of his nest, floating.

It's late afternoon when I got back to the cabin. I find a note from my wife in the door. I ignore the note, do nothing about dinner (it's too warm to light the cook stove), and make a campfire. I'm hungry. I eat the rest of the blackberries by the fire. Everyone deserves a second chance, and I forgive myself for what I'm about to do. It's raining again. I go into the cabin and listen to the rain, and raise a glass to the loons and the ravens, and to the next day when I plan to get sober again.

IMPOSTERS

⌒

I DON'T LEAVE THE NORTH COUNTRY from May
through July, but this year it's different because
my father's not taking his move to Florida well.
He spent most of his life in the little town on Long
Island where he and my mother raised me, and now
in a bungalow on the edge of a golf course he has
trouble sleeping—sometimes he doesn't remember
his new address. Before I leave, a letter arrives from
my father's girlfriend. There's odd behavior, she says,
the behavior of the aged. She threatens to "break
up" with him because, at seventy-three, she says (he's
eighty-two),there's better things to do than worry
through one crisis after another. (I don't ask what
these crises are; it shouldn't matter.) I get the letter,
then the phone call, on a day when all that Vermont

beauty seems suspended, the snow gone from the mountains, the air warm with spring . . . and then a solitary car ride through Blue Ridge Mountains, Carolina tobacco fields and Georgia swamps to my father's bungalow and the piles of beer cans, and his litany of reasons why he made a mistake moving south. Everything's different—even the spongy mat they call "lawn" and the violent sun. He can't even find his way through the Taj Mahal his girlfriend lives in to the bathroom.

My father says he feels out of his element. He's invisible.

Two weeks later, back in Vermont, I'll have carried my father's invisibility with me. Though I love my life in Vermont, I've always thought of myself as an imposter—you're not recognized as a native unless born here. Each of us, father and son, living as "invisibles" in a world not made for him.

In Vermont, driving the back roads looking for mulch hay, I'm surprised how few gardens have been planted, even at the farms in our valley. I stop in the driveway of a big white house with a sprawling porch, a tire hanging from a rope on a dead elm, a huge red barn, and walk around back where I'm greeted by a tail-wagging Rottweiler. A young man emerges from the milking parlor. He's got spoiled hay for the taking; though we've bumped into each other a number of times, he's not very friendly. I back up to the hay-barn door. Dirty light beneath the high rafters, shafts of hay dust—the dry scratch in my nostrils—and as I climb to the loft, the smell of it makes me dizzy.

I just returned from Florida, where I visited an old man who doesn't like it there even though he just arrived and hasn't given it a chance, and returning to my home place forces me to look up close at where I have lived. The pain of those earlier years in Vermont, when I was broke and jobless, has faded to a bittersweetness that says, "It never happened to you. You were always happy." But who am I to pretend that I am able to manage a woodpile, a garden, and house-mending? Even after living here three decades, I feel as though I've just arrived: the person who rises every morning at five to click away on his computer is as suited to living a "rustic" life as is his father to playing croquet in Florida. A sense of imposter-hood, that I'm not what I seem even to myself, is rooted in the demands of living on the land. I'm not up to those demands most of the time. Usually things go on fine without me. I put in our garden early this year—not by much, a few weeks, maybe—but it doesn't seem to make a difference. Tomatoes are never ripe before the end of July, and we don't have corn till September. The garden is on a plateau above our house where the soil's stoneless, loamy, with lots of sunlight. I found a good source of chicken manure at a neighboring farm—rich and black, mixed with sawdust-- and after I drove the bales home I got the manure, spread it liberally and went back for more. After I shoveled and delivered the shit, I thought about the farm I'd gotten the manure from, the little girl standing in burdocks watching me, a pair of red-eyed bulls black and white against the afternoon haze.

Suzanne had started everything six weeks before—tomatoes, broccoli, cabbage, cauliflower. She even had twenty tobacco plants, and echinacea, basil, parsley. She planted yarrow around our dog Sophie's grave at the end of the garden, trimmed the rose hips, planted a new clump of rhubarb and, after a long dry spell, it rained for two weeks and things grew lush and rank: raspberry bushes in profusion, burdocks wide-leafed as rhubarb wrestling for space. At first I'd liked the youthful competitiveness of it, then after all the heat and rain, the warm humid nights, there was a point where it all should have stopped.

What was wrong?

The canopy crowded out the sky three weeks earlier than usual, and late-spring clawed its way into my brain. Even the beauty, a cloying over-abundance, tightened its grip, making me look, *look*. And I listened to the highway traffic through the trees, a throat-clearing warble of veeries tremulous in the evening light, and then the scolding of a kingfisher, all of which prompted me to wonder why, after living in the deep woods so long, I felt this way about beauty.

∽

Mornings at my father's place, I walk along the golf course, following the arcing sprinklers and the early go-carts. There's a pair of early risers like myself and flocks of green birds in the trees. The sky is already mussed by smoke from the wildfires not far away: these last few days, the blaze spreads from north into central Florida. Route 95 is closed. Although it's rained for several days briefly in the afternoon, the wildfires have leapt from the piney woods into retirement country. Spaces open in the heat-curtain, and what's left of Florida's beauty fades. Smoke leaks into my father's girlfriend's house—into its three bathrooms, its radiating domes—and she dusts and dusts, but the smoke sifts through the walls. I'm staying alone in a motel in town. When he's able to negotiate the maze of avenues and cloverleafs from his little cottage to his girlfriend's palace, my father arrives there disheveled and confused with Mandy, my mother's toy poodle. He and I hardly talk. The silence that opens between us has smoldered for years. I'm aware of it most painfully when he doesn't answer me. The absent stare, his face going improbably blank. At such moments, I need to get away: one day, I drive north toward Gainsville and visit the house where Marjorie Kinnan Rawlings wrote *The Yearling*.

When I arrive in the hot late-afternoon, the house is closed up. I walk around the grounds beneath the tall oaks into a grove of orange trees. Not far away, a wide lake. A few chickens pecking around. A tom-cat on the long-eaved porch. Inside, I see Rawling's upright typewriter.

⌒

A while ago, our only neighbor and Suzanne and I put in a communal garden. Barry lives in an old homestead built by a group of hippies called "The Dreamers." Barry's the last of that original group. He tries to live as he did years ago, but he's become an attorney and spends more time on his computer than in his garden. The two gardens border each other, separated by pines. Barry's garden is overrun by milkweed and sumac. An old hippie school bus sits at the far end, and a few outbuildings from communal days crumble in the woods. Barry doesn't particularly like weeding, while I do: he also owns a rototiller, which I don't. We pooled our resources, made of our two plots one garden—but Barry's more interested in production than aesthetics, and his gardens look agri-cultural, industrial. We divided our tasks: Barry did the cultivating with his rototiller, I did the weeding. Suzanne and I, we're used to working alone, while Barry likes group activities. That's where our joint venture turned into a struggle over who would do what and who knew more about gardening. Over the years, we'd pushed each-others' vehicles out of snowdrifts, spent cozy winter evenings watching our battery-run tv. But working in the garden together was another thing. I felt no need to tend what wasn't mine. I wonder if this is the way friendships end, caving in from neglect.

We grew profligate in our neglect—we hated going to the garden. My friend took up bicycle riding, I bought a canoe and spent long afternoons in a nearby pond, and by the end of the summer, the "group garden" had turned to witch grass; the squash got lost in the undergrowth, the tomatoes turned to rot, melon and pepper plants went native and refused to bloom.

～

It's three days since I visited the garden: an equatorial rain. Manuscript pages curl on my desk. A lone potted cucumber on the porch yellows with dropsy. The chicken yard morassed in sleazy hay and chicken shit. An inhuman beauty burns off the hills—the raw prettiness of a canopy aglare in morning light. It's all intact save for this gardener: driving up the steep garden road, I hit a bump, my muffler falls off, and now my Ranger rumbles beneath me like a bellowing cow.

～

This business about beauty: enough of the quotidian enters in here that there's a buffer, an edge between me and "the good, true and beautiful." Life goes on—even side dressings of manure this hothouse summer seem superfluous as the storms roll over us, a lusty chorale of tropical lightning deflected off the hills. In the morning after the rains, I walk the garden perimeter—blackberry bushes crowd out the path; lambs' quarters grow insidiously along the margins. When I'm done the day's work, I sit on the porch and try to draw—the best sketches come naturally; the worst are awkward impersonations of art, and none of this is beautiful. Drawing a flower or a bush seems impossible—I can't capture any image, and even if I were a good draftsman, I'd have a hell of a time separating leaf and stem and branch. My mother, a fine graphic artist with an eye for texture and undertones, for those details that unmask—rather than hide—an object, could see into a thistle and make its prickliness come through your eyes into your other senses (how do you hear a thistle?). But she distanced nature from herself, and I can't imagine her with garden dirt on her hands, though there was always paint and ink beneath her fingernails.

Where I grew up, the only people I knew who had gardens were Italian and Polish immigrant families. Gardens weren't part of the Unitarian nature philosophy I'd been brought up in. I know several others like me raised Unitarian who retreated to a life in the woods. While the rest of the world staggered into the next century, we were moving backwards. Soon folks like my wife and I forgot why we'd come here. What was the purpose?

∽

It's hill country, Florida hill country. Scrub oak and horse country. The name of the retirement community is "Lady Lake," and indeed there's a lake on whose verges sit slinky condos and new mini-malls. The bungalows and retirement palaces done-up in fake adobe, Moroccan tile—subdued maroons, pale yellows, flamingo pinks—are found on Buena Vista

Drive, Camino Real Lane, Laredo Way. The view from my father's kitchen window takes in a golf course. A grid of power lines floats above the houses, a towering hex of energy. He keeps the radio on all day, and when the storms roll in, the kitchen roars with static. Bat-like insects splash against the windows. The air conditioner hums. My father's life may come to an end here, and that's what bothers him most—to be cast into Florida nothingness. Everything back home's been sold, the house, art studio, furniture. What made him move to Florida? The migratory urge of old age, the fact that he wants to start a new life apart from the past. What's left, he complains, is Florida. The golf course is ugly, save for a few snowy egrets wading in the ponds. And when it storms the sky glowers contentiously. To the east smoke smudges the horizon, and when the wind is off the ocean, the burnt-pine smell merges with the scent of barbecue.

North of Lady Lake, the Ocala horse ranches begin stretching to the palmetto hammocks of the Gulf coast. It's all scrub oak with occasional tall plane trees rising in the distance. Earth-stained pickups rumble down oyster-shell roads trailed by red dust. When I go driving, I take some of the back roads into man-icured racehorse land, which dips and rolls beneath the yellow grass. Split-rail fences and roan-colored horses and sumptuous country houses pass by, and then further west, the hills give out, the sun glares, the sawgrass shimmers, and the new highway buckles in the heat.

I drive through two worlds, two consciousnesses.

~

There were tall oaks around our house on Long Island, a scraggly front lawn, a blue pigeon coop out back, and a brook running through swamp cabbages to a drainage pipe. In the evening the pigeons circling around, lighting in the trees. The beauty lurked at the edges in the soft suburban light; late evening, the birds cooing in their coop, a foghorn hooted on the Sound. My friends and I would take our pigeons far out on the Island and release them, and they'd fly back home, miracles of navigation and telepathy. My love of animals—pigeons, specifically, and less ardently snakes, turtles—was more aesthetic than practical. I didn't know how hard it would be to live out my dreams, or how I'd outlive my dreams. I knew I wanted to move to the country, but I never knew what it would be like to actually live year after year in what is to others a savage ugly place—ten years carrying water from a hole cut in brook-ice for water in winter and as many summers slapping black flies, carting horse and chicken shit into an old poor farm garden, and years of sunny good health, running into a neurotic, heart-pounding fear. It was hard living in the woods without electricity or running water for more than a brief time, harder for my wife, who milked cows at a local farm, than for me because even in the worst times, I got a few courses at a nearby college. Our first gardens were hit-and-miss affairs, planted according to the wrong signs: some years the deer got what we put in before it had time to mature; other years frost and neglect killed off what we planted. Some of my own ancestors lived and were buried in southwestern Vermont and neighboring New York. It appears from their headstones—the last Whedon death dated 1816—that they deserted the state in the "year there was no summer," otherwise known as "eighteen-hundred and froze to death." Meteorological records show a frost in the area every month that year. It snowed in June and August (the crops were uniformly a disaster) and ash from volcanoes in Sumatra clouded the sky, splashing breathtaking sunsets across New England. The calamitous winter-in-summer along with those tragic sunsets bred apocalyptic thoughts in my ancestors, and moving west to Ohio and Nebraska—as did my wife's ancestors, who also lived in Vermont and left about the same time—would have been something like a religious pilgrimage for them.

But this old, poor farm garden—not a stone any-where; a hundred years ago they raised a quarter mile of potatoes here, and I've turned over horseshoes, barbed wire, various gardening tools—even some crockery shards and oxidized silverware. The garden still grows potatoes best. They like sandy, well-drained soil and the coolness that comes from the woods. This Spring, I tilled it three times, careful not to slide down an embankment into the woods. At least five acres, flat as a pond and sandy and well-drained, the plot ends abruptly at a cliff grown-over with sugar maple. At one end my wife planted rosehip bushes; at the other there's a patch of sun chokes, briars running into a logging road. The view through trees, around clouds gone amuck, fording those mountains. And a few weeks earlier, the truck conking out on River Road, a lane of home-bound traffic behind me—with a load of chicken shit in the bed, flies buzzing along the uncoiling river.

↜

When something goes wrong with my truck, I look into the engine, check alternator, battery connections, and fan belt while a voice hisses, "You've been driving second-hand heaps since you were a kid, and you'd think you'd have learned something." But it wasn't always this way. I was more the son of my mother than I was of my father. If my mother was here, I'd tell her an appreciation of views—garden views especially—is conditioned by the mind of the viewer. A postcard of a Vermont landscape isn't accompanied by birdsong, nor does it require three hours hoeing beans as a prerequisite for looking at it. My view through the woods on a July morning skirts the Trout River and is conditioned by the deer flies dive-bombing my head, and by the errata of memory. I try to recall how, for almost ten years, a life of necessity became one of relative indulgence. We sawed up dead beech and maple blowdowns, foraging from loggers' slash, even

though we didn't need to. We couldn't stop gardening, cutting wood for six months of .

⌐⟋

I arrive back from my brief trip to Rawlings' country
late in the evening. My father's cottage is empty, his car
is gone. The little dog Mandy doesn't yip and scratch
at the door like she usually does when I knock. I sit
in the grass out back watching the heat lightning, and
after an hour I drive to the girlfriend's house, where I
am greeted by the two of them in her driveway. I ask
where Mandy is, and my father doesn't answer. Finally,
his girlfriend says they put Mandy to sleep, she was too
much a burden for my father. I try to imagine what it
was, what crime the poodle committed. Now that the
dog's gone, though, there's little to hold my father to
the life he'd led. My father has been peeling off pieces
of himself, layer by layer, for months now, and what
he's left with I can't enter into. The unexpected has
become expected. The inexorable pounding heat, a
world combusting around him.

⌐⟋

The dream I had tonight was disarmingly simple:
I'm walking down the street where I grew up. In late
March, the earliest white flowers, snowbells, have
come up behind the porch. My mother shows me
them, and then she starts drawing in her sketch pad: I
watch them sprout on the page, fringed, curlicued—
brilliant. Her hands move furiously, filling in page
after page of her notebook.

Next morning Suzanne shows me her own hands, which are scratched from weeding the herb garden, her small wrists scratched from the weeding, the pruning, the cutting back of thistle and fireweed. I watch how she moves her hands when she talks, the smoothness, the grace of her gestures as she drinks her morning coffee, butters her muffin, glances out to where the sunlight is choked by the lush maples, and glances down to the chicken house where jewelweed and asters have bloomed.

On the ridge, a few birches have begun to change. There's in me an urgency that comes with the first chill nights, the expectation of frost. The days go by. The rains of mid-summer give way again to a Vermont-style drought. Leaves lose their luster. I'm awash in the desperate triteness of approaching fall.

I spend my last day in Florida helping my father sort out things from his last unpacked boxes. It seems use-less—no doubt "Lady Lake" is but a brief way station before he'll need supervised care. While there are signs of serious mental deterioration, he's snarly with me, impatient as ever, his face sunken, the whites of his eyes going yellow. I rummage through a carton of photo albums and a folio of reproductions of my mother's etchings, stacking them carefully, and a few moments later, I turn to see him toss the stack into a trashcan.

I'm back in Vermont and my father doesn't call. When I finally contact his girlfriend, I'm told he's in a local hospital, severely depressed, and I decide not to travel again to Florida, but make arrangements with a hospital social worker for her to meet with him, and I call his lawyer in Long Island to talk about legal matters. It's late summer. A few nights ago, we forgot to shut the door to the chicken house, and when I went down through the herb garden to the coop, I heard the chickens squawking and the unmistakable chit-chat of coons. I poked in my flashlight: on the floor were eight baby coons munching on grain, while fifteen hens and a rooster peered down at them, expecting that they'd be the next course. Suzanne was not far behind. She grabbed a broom and began swatting, and the coons cowered behind the feed and water buckets, and hid their faces with their little clawed hands. So charming—and maybe dangerously rabid—one by one, they exited the coop, swollen bellied, drunk with laying mash.

The garden hasn't been weeded in a week. I interplanted cucumbers and squash with the corn, and the spaces between the cornrows are impenetrable, the cukes climbing the tall stalks, weighing them down. It's all a patternless, rangy, choking slurry of green. Deer tracks on the garden's edge. Crows heading for home. I think of my father at dusk. Thoughts that have no shape, no real content. They are premonitions, dark, textury, pigeons circling through the trees, the sound of whose voice calling down the years?

A breakdown in communication, the social worker says, nothing more, returning my calls three days, a week, late. Your father is still grieving over your mother's death, she says, and I imagine her, a small woman with crinkly sunburnt skin and sun-bleached hair.

Three in the morning, half in a dream, I'm back at home on Long Island: the little eddies of normalcy on our block are framed by lime green lawns, hollyhocks and hydrangeas, by swooping willow trees and creaking porch swings. Mornings, I'd wake to the sound of the retired butler next door clearing his throat. I'd look out and see Jones, tall and balding with a hank of dove-white hair in back, troweling into the dirt beneath a porch trellis.

Where's my father in all this? Why can't I remember him?

I dream of my own tea-house, my own retirement house.

High on a hill in our glacier-scoured valley.

I'd make a path out of brook stones and plant scores of purple irises in the little clearing. The tea-house would have a tri-cornered roof, no walls to obstruct the view, and the floors would be cut from native hemlocks, knotted and gnarly, burnished by our bare feet. I'd paint the roof beams orange. In the fall, when we could see through the trees, we'd watch the geese migrate and the hills darken with snow.

DEER PARK

⤳

THE END OF ANOTHER SLEEPLESS NIGHT and I'm out of the house, armed with a twelve-gauge, heading up through the hemlock woods to the garden. While I've been busy with an early harvest and devising ways to keep critters out of the fall seedlings, I've ignored the larger life around me, including the hemlocks, companions most of my life. This dank morning, the forest seems alien to me. That line from the old song, "I talk to the trees but they don't listen to me," suggests a ridiculous egotism I hope I don't represent here. I hear the trees talking in low, whispering tones, but my talking to them is, well, inconsequential.

The northern forest has always been considered a holy place. German theologian Rudolph Otto maps out the aesthetics of it in his book, *The Idea of the Holy.* "The semi-darkness," Otto writes, "that glimmers in vaulted halls or beneath the branches of a lofty forest glade, strangely quickened and stirred by the mysterious play of half-lights, has always spoken eloquently to the soul." Otto says that, to have a mystical effect, the forest darkness must contrast with a flickering or dying light. I wonder if what we dub "mystical"—the *mysterium tremendum* experienced in old-growth forests—isn't just the awe of contemplating primordial survivors. The hemlocks around my garden aren't so much relics of that past as they are ghosts of it. And if ghosts are memories floating loose from bodies that once owned them, then these trees carry memories of long gone snow storms and blistering droughts beyond written history.

I'm through the apple and cherry orchard, into the plummy dawn light. No critter—no woodchuck, coon or porcupine— yet just the ooze of deep woods silence. Part of me feels linked to this forest while another is disconnected. I want the hemlocks to be transcendent, but that's a human wish. They wish the darkness were darker, that their broken branches would mend, and that their lives' possum-slow curve would be even slower. No doubt, they communicate with each other, but each thought takes months, years, to be expressed. They tell each other stories beyond words, with no end. There's no irony, no humor in their stories, but there is agreement that time is memory, that without memory they're no more than bark-encased impulses of tree sap.

I lay my poncho on a rise of ground a few yards into the woods with a full view of the garden. A jay flaps up from his tamarack roost; and then more silence. There's yellow, crumbling porcupine shit, piles of it, scattered along the now-rusted barbed wire we strung up twenty years ago to keep out the neighbor's cow, with a few faded winter prints of deer trucking uphill toward the meadow.

And the sorghum scent of late-summer.

Otto's The Idea of the Holy implies that God isn't worth a pile of porcupine shit if He doesn't provoke knee-knocking dread. The attributes of Otto's mystical experience include his sense of God's unapproachability, His power to humble and His wrathfulness. Our hemlock grove provokes in me a mystical wonder—how couldn't it?—based on my intimacy with the woods' moods and an awareness of its teeming particulars. Each day, these hemlock groves say something different. After a blizzard, their boughs shake off their snowy burden and shiver with delight; following a heavy rain, they rise like intertwined phantoms in the mist. The mood of the woods sparks an awe in me distinct from the fear that Otto says comes from the forest's "unapproachability." Fear comes from ignorance. Otto's Calvinism, the kind our Puritans brought to the New World, mistakes ignorance for humility.

The concept of an unknowable God and an unknowable Nature dates back to Old Testament times, in the barrens of the Arabian Peninsula, when the Desert

Fathers had nothing but a cloudless sky as their companion. Constantly in fear of nameless hazards beyond a huge horizon, it was natural for the Jews to conceive a fearsome God. As part of a goat-herding culture, they and their Berber brethren contributed to the desiccation of the ancient Middle East and North Africa. Only the Bible's earliest verses, its proverbs and songs, celebrate the richness of Nature, and here they dwell on agricultural cycles, not on complex interactions between humans and the wild (leave that to the T'aoists, writing their Book of Changes at the same time the early biblical yarns were assembled). No wonder God was fashioned in a wanderer's image! No wonder He was One God! (No room for pantheism if there's nothing to pantheize.) Eco-archaeologists tell us that, by 1,000 BC, much of the grassy savannah was over-grazed, so Semitic herdsman wandered a desert of their own making. Nomads, they wouldn't have had much stake in one place: a dread of what was beyond the next dune, a fear of an unknowable, wrathful God who represented the opposite of plentiful multiplicity, would have ruled them.

Fear of the void has dogged descendants of the desert tribes ever after. But there's not much of nothing—no empty horizon, no duney wastes—in the hemlocks, numinous and mystical though they are. They give us more opportunities for delight than occasions for dread. Ask any bird watcher. It's as important for us to learn the names of birds—the wood thrushes and veeries, the spruce grouses (rarer each year), the finches and redstarts and the red-tail hawks—as it is for a hoary-bearded Old Man to have named them. And it must be a sin, has to be sin, not to take delight in them.

~

This spring I planted fifteen apple, cherry, and pear trees, half of which have been nibbled at by deer. I'm more familiar with the habits of deer than with fruit trees. After they stripped most of the leaves from our Macs, I put up fencing which seems to have done the trick. I see few deer in Summer, but they're here this morning. Deeper into the woods, there's more deer pellets and a mess of tracks through the hemlocks to our garden. Cool in summer, warm in winter, the hemlock grove is my Deer Park, a Middle Way between seasonal extremes. Late-July rain light falls through the forest, an Arcadian light suggesting lost summers and summers yet to be. In youth, the hemlocks have a slender grace, but as they mature from a sooty tan to earthy browns, their bark shags and thickens and they contort into humanoid shapes. Willows and birch have supple shapes, but when hemlocks grow old they get grotesque, even gargoyle-like. It's not unusual to find some in our old-growth forest living 800 years.

For millennia, the whitetail that yard up in the hemlocks have used the same trails, one following the ridge of a ravine above our house, another crossing the sloping land straight to the orchard and around the garden. Deer are our hemlocks' age-old companions: their shit fertilizes them, their nibbling keeps undergrowth down. Hemlocks also enjoy the company of sugar maples, yellow birch and an occasional ironwood all of which like shallow, damp, but well-drained soil. Several things help hemlocks survive—they hold out well against forest fires and disease. They are knotty, splinter easily and are not of much use for lumber—railroad ties come from hemlock, but when was the last time a new railroad line was built anywhere? Hemlocks are cut to make boxes and crates and are used in rough-cut construction. The toughest of the softwoods—splitting a gnarly hemlock's about as hard as splitting beech or maple—they are doggedly persistent, taking forever to reach maturity.

Proof that hemlocks lived here longer than white folks can be found in their hummock remains on the forest floor; but you seldom see a fresh hemlock blow-down, much less one felled by old age. The centuries-old, hundred-and-twenty footer that crashed down near our house many years ago will take another thirty years to turn to humus. For now, it's home to squirrels, a feast for insects and grub-eating birds. A clearing naturally forms around that old fellow honoring his demise. White birch, the jazziest trees of the northern forest (there's a line of them at the edge of my garden), look like they're swooning while the hemlocks lean gently into each other, in a millennial conversation.

In early spring, before the hemlock canopy is filled out by leaves of the sugar maple and yellow birch, the forest floor comes alive with trout lilies, "spring beauties" and trillium. Soon, the dappled trout lilies sprout tiny, bell-like yellow flowers and the stinky, garishly red-petaled trillium transform into jack-in-the-pulpits. All this happens just after the snow disappears. Snowmelt runs into low spots between hummocks to form vernal pools that breed frogs and our first mosquitoes. Several varieties of fern then shoot up and unfurl, and as the forest floor falls into summer shadow, the spring flowers fade away.

Our hemlock forest undulates up the valley following a brook into the mountains. There's a quick cutoff between hemlocks and other trees. You can tell where the old timers farmed—where the hardwoods begin. Farther up the mountain, a windbreak of white pine honors the Conservation Corps of the 1930s. Just behind the tall rows of pine, crumbling homestead foundations hide in the crowding undergrowth and mark the farthest reaches of hemlock. There on up the mountain, it's maple and birch, some still saplings, and then red spruce and elevation-stunted beech and ash. You can map water courses by tracing the reach of hemlocks along the brooks and deep, bedded rivers in our walled-in valley. The brook descends in waterfall after waterfall, pools forming between them where brook trout reside, one big trout in each little pond. The dense hemlock shade keeps the trout waters cool in summer—sunlight won't seep through the trees until mid-day when the trout start feeding. The Abenaki Indians drank hemlock bark tea for colds, fever, diarrhea, and other ailments, and there's reason to believe that the brook water we drink, filtered through the sand and gravel of a cistern bordering our brook, is tinctured with hemlock.

In our northern reaches, hemlocks can rise 150 feet from root to crown. Like most tall conifers, on each tier of branches thrive a volary of conifer-loving birds. These include white- and red-winged cross-bills, who eat the hemlocks' little cones by crushing them with pincer-like beaks, and all manner of warblers, finches, grosbeaks and boreal chickadees, pine siskins, and purple throated hummingbirds. A pair of red tail hawks return each year to the same nest in one of our tallest hemlocks. They've built a big nest midway up and perch in the treetops to check out their territory.

By April, after a month's gestation, the fledglings venture out, plunging and veering, honing their hunting skills while they play. And they are playful birds, vocal too, especially in Spring and early Summer when the parents keep a watchful eye on them. Up and down our valley meadow to meadow they go, soaring in wide circles for the longest time. The red tail's unmistakable *kee-ree, kee-ree* is often dubbed into movies to simulate the sounds of eagles: these hawks are to eagles as our hemlocks are to the redwoods—less majestic, but in synch with our landscape's intimate scale. Still, with a wing span of 53 inches, the red tail is the largest North American hawk. Though it weighs just two pounds, it's known to kill and eat house cats, skunks, porcupines, and woodchucks several times its weight. Spotting its prey with binocular vision from a tree, it takes off with powerful wing beats, then glides to the ground and strikes, legs doubled up under the force of a hard impact that automatically clenches the birds' toes and talons, piercing their victim's inner organs.

Yesterday, I saw a red tail perched atop a dead hemlock above our garden. It peered down at the rows of beans and tomato plants, on the lookout for woodchucks, I suppose. In recent years there's been an uptick in the rodent population. It triggered an increase in red tails. During this period, my garden was plundered by woodchucks, moles, and mice. I thought to plant a garden down the ravine nearer our house, but, lazy, I stayed put. Now, the end of July, nothing has been chewed at save the young cabbages in a late-season slug infestation.

Hemlocks are targets for snowshoe hare that nibble the seedlings and strip bark from the younger trees. Very little sunlight seeps through the canopy, so there's not much of an understory and little brush for the rabbits to hide in. Even so, when snowshoes return to our area as they do in decade-long cycles, more predators like the red tails, barred owls, and a few Canadian lynx wander in. Lynx feed exclusively on hares, unlike their omni-carnivorous bobcat cousins. Several years ago, in an August drought at the peak of a snowshoe cycle, my wife and I watched a lynx drinking at our brook. It stood at the edge of a pool, still as a stuffed animal. For a moment, we thought it was stuffed.

How to reconcile the lynx's tawny stillness, its quiet watchfulness, with the busy-ness of the hemlock forest? At this time of year, late-July, there's still some territorial chatter left over from early summer. At dusk, the thrushes' song becomes a ruminative murmur. With the last heavy spring rains a memory, the brook listlessly grumbles.

⸐

Actually, it rained all last night. It is still raining. This morning the woods are as dark as a Robert Frost poem, but at the edge of the hemlocks where deciduous trees take over, bands of sunlight stream in. Deeper into the birch and maple, the ground cover thickens with lilies of the valley. This spring I picked wild leeks here under a big sugar maple, and along the stream bank, fiddleheads and wild salad greens.

The wildflower beds have vanished, and it's raining again, a warm, late-July rain streaming down the hemlocks. Cinnamon colored, tannin-stained rain in the diffused light. Tannins come from the bark of any tree, but are especially potent in evergreens. They're also astringent. Chew some hemlock bark and your cheeks pucker. Poultice a bee sting with hemlock

bark and its tannins draw out the venom. Trappers
and shoemakers use tannin to cure leather and kill
bacteria. They're great for body tanning, and are
found in non-herbal teas. If you drink the rainwater
from the pools around these hemlocks, your insides
will pucker and turn Ceylon tea-brown. No theo-
logical text discusses the soul's in-drawing caused by a
micro-quivering of one's nostrils at the styptic aroma
of evergreen needles and bark. After a rain, when the
hemlocks' pheromones are released into the air, the
soul congeals to the size of a blueberry. The odor is
woody and vinegary.

After this, Jesus knowing all things were accom-
plished, that the scripture might be fulfilled, saith, I
thirst. Now there was set a vessel full of vinegar: and
they filled a sponge with vinegar, and put upon it
hyssop, and put it to his mouth. When Jesus therefore
had received the vinegar, he said, It is finished: and he
bowed his head, and gave up the ghost.

It's not just fortuitous that the vinegar-soaked
sponge forced into Jesus' mouth has hyssop placed
upon it. *Hyssop*, a word of Greek origin, was named
from *azob*, an evergreen herb, because it was used to
clean holy places. It is alluded to in the scriptures:
"Purge me with hyssops, and I shall be clean." Known
for its healing virtues, hyssop was drunk by the ancients
in a tea as an expectorant and a stimulant, and would
have had a bitterly ironic significance to Jesus' follow-
ers as it was also used to paint the doorposts of Jewish
homes with lamb's blood during Passover. There's an

astringent finality to Jesus' giving up, just as there is a diminishment of one's ego in the midst of hemlocks whose sharp scent forces one conversely—and involuntarily—to be drawn out of oneself. Wine vinegar and hyssop were the last things Jesus tasted on earth.

First and last things merge in hemlock groves. Often their deep melancholy makes me feel like the last person on earth.

Sometimes, after a rain or a snowstorm, I'm revived. The hemlocks' shadows and their acidic scent, not unlike that of incense, and their primal silences stimulate mindfulness. Hemlock groves are acoustical dead zones. Ferns and sphagnum moss carpeting the dampish floor baffles and dampens sounds. Were the hemlocks to have a grammar, it would be punctually declarative, but if they spoke it wouldn't be in Latin. Their language is the raw demotic of country bumpkins. Now in midsummer, the plangent teacher, teacher of oven birds. Their dour Franciscan habits proclaim a message of compassion to all living creatures. When I walk in the redwoods, I feel like I've gone to heaven. But the hemlocks are purgatorial. Some trees raise me up and make me shout "Lordy," but a hemlock grove elicits no more than a murmur.

No better way to temper greedy excess than with a few gulps of hemlock tea.

Socrates committed suicide by drinking a noxious herbal infusion from central Asia, not the same hemlock as the subject of this essay. This hemlock grove seems a good enough place to die in, to make one's peace in, or to tell the truth in. The sounds are muted, the light subdued, as the music of rain drips through the trees. Like many people, I fear dying in a hospital room, monitors bleeping. I'd prefer an old-fashioned death attended by farmers and farm wives, farriers, and mill workers whose stories of making-do in bone-cold winters, of infant death and home burials, whose delight in the unexpected warmth of a February day are truths enough for me.

⤺

Why do I delight in them? Maybe delight is too strong a word. Rapture—the born-again kind—is even stronger, way too strong. Rapture blows your heart open, but delight opens your eyes a bit wider. You can be enraptured, but not en-delighted. You feel delight in the company of a good friend and rapture in the midst of a go-for-broke love affair. Rapture's shadow is Despair, but Delight's anti-self is sweet Melancholy. Delight sparkles and scintillates, and Rapture smokes and smolders. You get too much Rapture and you're headed for a psychiatrist's office, but there's no such thing as too much Delight, too much of an essentially good thing. I delight in the hemlocks, because they are what they intend to be. In today's Summer rain, I hear the hearty thwack of a pileated woodpecker knocking himself senseless somewhere in the forest. Despite the rain, or maybe because of it, there's a lot of foolery in the hemlocks, goldfinches giddy on thistle seeds, a kingfisher rattling up Dreamers Brook.

I make my way past a maple blown down in last week's windstorm. And through raspberry patches and up into an open meadow where more rain clouds greet me.

SIDEMAN

⌒

"I want to be a sideman, just an ordinary sideman ..."

—DAVE FRISCHBERG

THE PAIN JUST ABOVE HIS GROIN is strongest after he eats or when he's stressed, and these days he's stressed all the time. It happens after he has a few drinks, or fought with his ex, or talked to his daughter, or if he's gotten up way too early to sub-teach, which he's done all this year. They call him because he shows up and is dependable, but today the pain's more intense, because his car got sideswiped on the street by a hit-and-run and he hasn't the bread to pay for another won't have the means to get to school, doesn't have the cash for cab fare, and there's nothing but last night's half-smoked reefer on the kitchen table. He owes the landlord two years' back rent. He owes his dentist who fitted his dentures. But mostly, he thinks of his little girl with end-stage bladder cancer. Before that she had leukemia and went through years of chemo, then back in January she began peeing blood and they knew they were in for it again. He'd stayed in south Florida, where they lived during her first illness, and taught at the U. of Miami: his chops were good, he had more gigs than he could handle, and he played like no one ever has: compare him to Woody Shaw, his runs were like Woody's, the way he blurred one note into another was like Don Cherry; but there was a design to how he played. He was lyrical like Chet, and like Chet he told a musical story, but something lurked at the margin of his playing, haunting but beautiful, and he wondered if his daughter, Ginger, had something to do with it.

Now winter light skates in the smudged window. He sees the Volvo in the driveway (defunct), the morning traffic on Winooski, and a few errant flurries in the air as a flock of Somali girls in their exotic headgear flit by. The phone rings. The caller ID tells him it's the school calling, but there's no way to get anywhere. He lights the reefer. He puts on some Mahler and, leaning back, thinks he might just hole up in his room and drink himself stupid. There's that song "Alfie" about a dude who's overdone it like he did, about the possibility of loving just one woman, Alfie, what the fuck are you doing in Winooski, Vermont? In Miami, he visited Ginger, bald and scarily underweight in her hospital bed, the chemo going into her and all the waste of life draining out. When she was well enough, they lived on an artificial island his wife's old man owned in the Keys, and when Ginger was strong again, he left her with Gretchen while he gigged elsewhere: it was prime time in his career; he'd refined his mature style and was getting known, but the bread from work even with high-profile bands was problematic. There was the reminder, too, of his daughter: her health was sketchy, provisional. The trouble began six months ago, when she screamed for her mother about the blood in her urine. They'd been living, Ginger, Gretchen, and him, in a house Gretchen bought in a nowhere part of the state. Gretchen was a loner and she needed isolation, but she was a mall-girl too and she liked to shop, and there were no shops up there. He slept in a rebuilt horse barn with tall, schoolhouse windows facing a weedy pond; at night he cooked them three-course gourmet meals and, between Gretchen and him, they put away a couple of bottles of wine. Thus began the good life away from the city, the lonely nights driving back to Gretchen's in snowstorms, the ridiculous lonely mornings trying to keep his chops in shape.

The Mahler drifts up from the carpet into the finale, the piano restating the Quartet in A Minor's theme, the three strings and the keyboard dark and lofty enough for today. Mahler wrote the piece at age fifteen, and it swooned the way an adolescent swoons. Like him, Mahler had been a dandy, what they called a boulevardiere, grandiose in everything he composed, even the quartet (rare in Mahler's opus). His affinity for Mahler had as much to do with the belle epoch—Mahler's time—as it did with the music. Gretchen accused him of fancying himself a figure out of some fin-de-siecle fairytale, but he couldn't help being born in the wrong century.

Last month, he did a three-day teaching stint with Joe Lovano at McGill in Montreal, and, broke now, he's still waiting for his "honorarium" to come in. He'd known Kevin Dean from the McGill University Jazz Program, from when they both taught at a jazz camp: the McGill gig was a relief from Vermont, a chance to hang with his friend Joe from the Woody Herman days. They were asked to lecture on "finding a voice." Barry's voice came from the mistakes he'd made over the years, and from his father's Charlie Shavers, Roy Eldridge, and Buck Clayton records and his father's swing band. To have a voice you had to grow up with the music, you had to listen to Kenny Dorham, Clifford Brown, and Bird till your ears fell off. You needed to put everything into your horn and confess to it your most earnest weaknesses.

The students had known Barry'd played with Gerry Mulligan and Horace Silver, and Joe Lovano's Nonet, which meant little or nothing to them. Joe showed off a crazy new tenor with a double bell he blew while Barry played drums and trumpet on "All the Things You Are," Joe taking the lead while he blew arpeggios around the melody. After they finished, someone asked if Barry was post-Newtonian—there wasn't any specific gravity to his playing—and he'd said: how the hell could you have a "voice" if all you did was show off what it was impossibly not? Voice wasn't style. That came from the swagger you projected. Voice was what you were left with when you put the horn down. To understand his playing, you had to come to it with the history of jazz, all the bumps and grinds of it, under your belt, Joe said, you had to know Barry had established his own voice and fresh new ideas about what trumpet playing could be.

He went to the fridge. He withdrew a Heineken he'd left there last night. The sight of greasy chicken legs and day-old pasta ignited the pain in his groin, and he sat down with the bottle and toyed with his mouthpiece, thinking about Lovano. They'd both grown up in Ohio. Joe came from a rambunctious Sicilian brood (his father had been a tenor player), and by age fifteen, he had learned the changes to all the tunes. Barry had played trumpet and drums in his father's band, accounting for why his trumpet sounded rhythmic and his drumming was near-harmonic. He remembered the VFW bar his father's band gigged in as much the tunes they played—"If I had You," "Moonglow"—and he remembered the vets on the dance floor talking about anything but the Vietnam War and how they hadn't won it. He'd picked up an affinity for black people and their music, and after he left college at North Texas State, he gigged with black bands. By then white musicians had turned against blacks and vice-versa.

But the black guys he played with appreciated his playing, they liked him. Once with Horace Silver, he experienced reverse discrimination when a bar owner threatened to cancel if Horace didn't get rid of the white trumpet player, but Horace had stood up for Barry. He still had a foggy photo taken of him and the four other musicians that night. He'd been married to a black girl who stood at the edge of the photograph, inexplicably giving Horace the finger. He'd shown the picture to his father, who didn't like black people, just to piss him off, but the old man had slipped into dementia by then.

After the lecture, he'd gone back to his hotel and sat on the balcony watching the traffic: it was snowing in Montreal, and the city was brilliant and white. He wandered into the lobby, bought a pack of Canadian cigarettes and chatted up the desk girl, who pretended she knew who he was. He had a gig at the jazz bar Upstairs and asked if she'd join him for a drink later, and she said she would. Back in his room, he smoked a joint. He fell asleep on the balcony in the snow and dreamed about Ginger, who the desk girl reminded him of.

Montreal is a little like New York with Paris thrown in. It's lit up like Paris and built on an island like Manhattan, but tonight Montreal was windy and forbidding. He blew into his mouthpiece while the snow fell down, and when it was time, he went down to the street. The gig started at nine-thirty, and he was late. He got into a cab; he watched the nightlife drift by, and thought about how untrained the McGill kids were—mention Bix or Louis or Dizz, and they had no idea what you were talking about. The cabby, who spoke no English, drove him down into Montreal's Old Town, into a seedier part of the city, arriving after several deliberate wrong turns late. The room was filled with McGill kids waiting for him to step on his dick, and for a time, his teeth felt loose and the rhythm section rushed the beat.

Trying to lose some weight, Joe had walked down ten blocks from McGill to hear his old friend; now he sat at a table waiting to sit in. Joe never grew tired of hearing Barry, because what counted weren't Barry's mistakes, which weren't actual mistakes but trips to the ragged edge of things. Even though his teeth were loose, he snagged a few high notes; then he relaxed, and became his old self, knowing that if you were out of shape you had to play fast, go for broke.

After the first set, his teeth felt tight. He saw Joe had come by. Kevin Dean from McGill was there too, and behind Kevin, a table full of Asian girls cheered the band on. The rhythm section was altogether creditable, and things went from smooth to exciting, then to exhilarating, and the next set when Joe sat in it felt marvelous. The first tune they played, "Invitation," was vigorous, unison playing, the two sharing the melody and falling sweetly asunder at the release.

⌣

Much writing about jazz focuses on overdoses and colorful pratfalls. It depends on hearsay and apocrypha, and it verges on hagiography. But there's no saints in jazz, only unredeemed sinners—that's why it's hard to come to terms with the music. There's much romancing of drugs in jazz stories, but more important to Barry's playing was what he read—he reads voraciously—and his tastes in women. He's a non-stop raconteur, and his story-telling enters the music. If there's a problem, it's that he calls attention to himself by preening and clowning, of which there's lots of precedents in jazz.

In high school, he'd pitched for a baseball team, and his coach had pushed him toward a ballplaying career. By then he was deep into the music. He feared losing his front teeth with a fastball to the mouth, and to his coach's regret, he'd quit the team. Coach had tried to lure him back, saying he'd been missing out on good pussy if he quit. It was true that being a star pitcher had allure; playing trumpet did too, but he'd never been a star, just a sideman. A bona fide sideman is what he was.

A couple of weeks after Montreal, he took Ginger to England on a two-week Lovano gig at Ronnie Scott's in London. Ginger wore a two-thousand dollar wig, a crimson dress, a pearl necklace, and gold lame shoes, and everyone thought she was Barry's girl. Dennis Irwin was playing bass: a year later, he'd die of bone cancer, and Ginger would die too. But in London they were both alive. They went to the London Museum, saw the Elgin Marbles. They took a boat ride down the Thames, and watched the changing of the guard, and shopped on Fleet Street (where in one afternoon she spent everything he'd earned at Ronnie Scott's), and sitting in Kew Gardens in the rain, they talked about what Ginger's life would be like after she got well again. They stayed in London a week after the gig to take in the sights, and he got a one-nighter with a trio at a pub near Trafalgar Square, an upscale dive whose owner told the musicians not to drink on the job. That last night, in a low neckline purple dress, Ginger looked elegant and sophisticated, and he was so happy he had a whisky.

He played a set with the trio, drank another, and the pub owner, a West Indian, refused to let him back on the stand. Though Ginger had seen him let loose before, even by his own standards he reacted violently, kicking over their table and staining her decollete with cocktail sauce, and the bouncer escorted them out.

They took an early flight next day back to New York. Ginger was silent the whole way. Somewhere over the Atlantic, they hit some turbulence that knocked a flight attendant to her knees, slammed open overhead compartments, and for a flickering moment, dimmed the lights. He was terrified. They landed at Kennedy unharmed, and he got a rent-a-car and drove an unforgiving Ginger to Connecticut. Then he drove back to Vermont.

"You play for yourself first," Bill Evans has said. "You don't embroider, you don't make people work hard to hear what you're playing, but try to reveal something in yourself." The trick wasn't playing the right note, but finding the right space and the right silence and finding the note you refused to play. As he grew older, he'd gotten to appreciate lesser musicians—he enjoyed hearing the young cats do their thing. At the same time, he was more critical of his own work. Whether anyone else liked what he did wasn't the point—he had his standards. These included creating the illusion of effortlessness: that the notes he tried for he didn't strive for. That's to say, he was no Cat Anderson or Doc Severinsen, but blew solos that depended on imagination and lyrical clarity to carry him through.

Someone famous has said jazz means "fuck you." That was a 'black thing' coming out of Jim Crow and the refusal—that resounding NO—meant saying NO to the affirmative. The paradox was that the non-affirmative players, the nihilists who had nothing to lose—the Ben Websters, Art Peppers, and Chet Bakers—were the most lyrical. He thought back to the lecture on "voice" he and Joe had given at McGill. What they hadn't said was that voice came out of silence. Dizzy had said, "Jazz is the spaces between the notes." He'd go on to say the spaces themselves had meaning.

It's not ironic that, in the months before Ginger's death, his trumpet and drumming began to improve. Whether others heard it didn't matter—the late night stands in smoky mill towns, the logging trucks passing him on the way home on snowy mountain roads, the women he failed pick up in the joints where he played, they were all part of his music, as were the semi-literate kids he taught when he subbed in the schools. It was the sinking feeling he had when, weary from a night's playing, he stopped off at a diner and rapped with the counter girl.

It's going too far to say that what he read entered his music in more than a circuitous way, but music helped to understand what he read. He was turning the last page of Balzac's *Lost Illusions,* the story of a young poet who tries desperately to make a name for himself in Paris, but who discards his poetic aspirations and turns to hack journalism and descends into Parisian low life, leading to his own death, when Gretchen called from Connecticut. She and Ginger had moved there to be near Sloane Kettering, where she went for more tests. Ginger had taken a bad turn, and the docs had given her two months to live. He decided that, if he didn't talk about her being terminal, she'd stay alive.

Instead of heading straight-away to New York, he procrastinated. He took a bus into Burlington and walked around, peering into shop windows and feeling sorry for himself. He'd called a woman friend to front him till he got over this hump in his life. They planned to meet outside a Euro-style bar where he'd played a year before, and he sat at a table. The woman lived in a splashy house on the lake filled with African wood carvings and old jazz records, and she liked to talk about music and books, but he couldn't recall her face or name.

When she rounded a corner in her sunglasses and well-coiffed gray hair, he remembered it was Esther.

Esther offered him a clove cigarette.

"What is it now, Barry?"

"Jesus Esther, don't look at me that way," he said.

He had one or two wealthy doctors and dentists who helped him out. The dentist who'd made and fit his dentures was one. Presently, Esther was one too. He told her he had only twenty minutes before he had to head to the university, where he'd ask for work: she said she wanted to catch him that night at a Burlington club. She loved when he held his horn with one hand and worked the high hat and snare with the other. It was goddamn phallic.

Last week, he said, he'd called the university looking for work, but he was beaten out by a Latino trumpet player. The guy had a ten-year-old boy with cancer the same shape as Ginger was in, and while he felt for the guy, he planned to corner him for a teaching gig. He had nothing against the faculty, but most academics couldn't play shit if not in The Real Book. The dude—a spirited Puerto Rican trumpet player with more chops than Barry had—didn't fit in that category, but a potential university gig qualified him to be hit on. (Not long ago, musicians thrived off female patrons—Chopin had George Sands, Monk and Bird had their New Jersey Countess.) He borrowed another cigarette from Esther and drew his hand back before she could grasp it, and next morning, he took an Amtrak down to the city.

～

In Manhattan, he picked up a gig at a Chinese restaurant, booked by a stockbroker who paid the band out of pocket, after which he and the guitar player debouched to an after-hours joint where the clientele lay around like stoned pashas and musicians coming from earlier gigs played till five in the morning. Leaving the club, they witnessed a murky dawn over Westchester Avenue. The Elevated was running. The street swarmed with head-scarfed immigrants reminding him of Winooski. At a coffee shop across from a funeral home, he sat with the guitar player looking across at the undertaker sign. The guitar player told him he'd always been like this—for Barry the glass was always half-empty, never half-full.

He rode the IRT down to Sloane-Kettering. Gretchen had been there all night. Maybe it was the moon, the fucking moon and stars, but since he went to Vermont nothing went right, he told Gretchen. He had no self-pride, but just sat around waiting for the gigs to roll in, nursing the ache in his groin. "What kind of a goddamn life is that, Barry?" Gretchen said when they went out to smoke.

"It's the only one I have," he said.

They went back to Ginger's room. She was asleep, the covers pulled up to her chin, her skin translucent as smoked glass.

⌒

One of his great pleasures was Christmas.

He was a chump for songs of the season. The smarmiest Christmas tunes—the old Crosby numbers "White Christmas" and "The Little Drummer Boy"—made his eyes water. Otherwise, he was an un-sentimentalist. For years, he hadn't been in love, the idea of it made his stomach churn, but his German heritage, the "Old Tannenbaum" in him, carried him away: he loved the Charlie Brown Christmas tunes and made a point of caroling with Gretchen and Ginger. In front of a roaring fire, they'd go through a yuletide songbook and read "The Night Before Christmas."

So it was tragic and sad when she passed away a few days before Christmas.

He called me from Connecticut two hours after her death. "We lost her, we just lost her," he said, and I knew he wouldn't return to Vermont. In the next weeks, he became increasingly angry. He got by for a few days by on Ginger's leftover painkillers and nursed a score of resentments against Vermont folks he knew. He went to a clinic and got the pain in his groin checked out: his blood tests were negative— your liver is fine, the colon is fine, and you're not diabetic, they said—and he had nothing but his grief for his daughter to fall back on.

I'd met him three years back through Dan Silverman, a trombone-player friend of mine and Joe Lovano's brother-in-law. Joe had alerted Dan that Barry had come to Vermont and asked him to get him some gigs, make him at home in alien territory and remind him he had to eat. We played scores of gigs and became close, and I bailed him out when I could, got him gigs and fed him up.

After he hung up (sobbing), I called Tom Fay, a pianist friend who'd played with Barry in the Mulligan band and had gigged with the two of us in Vermont. Our talk moved to Barry and their days with Mulligan. To Tom, Barry was just another sideman with more talent than he knew what to do with. "But you should know," he said, "that the one time I played with Barry with you, it was his drumming that really impressed me. In fact, the way he used space and texture and contrast has become a kind of model for me. He is, I think, the first drummer I've ever known with almost no traditional drumming technique to play the instrument so that it really works. I'm not articulating that well. But when I am adding drums to my shit (Tom is recording his keyboard over a synthesized drum track) it's Barry's sound that I try to emulate—at least my memory version of it."

I haven't said much about his drumming, though that's how I know him best: at the Montreal club where I heard Lovano and Barry a year ago, Joe remarked to me that most drummers, even the good ones, play drums, but they're not musicians. It took awhile to let this sink in.

～

Ginger died in December, leaving Barry bereft. Yet the notes kept coming, the music blew out of him while he was angrier than when we first met. Mingus had that anger, Ben Webster did, too. Mingus got bolder, even more inventive, as he aged, and Webster's whisky tenor took on a deep amber tone, and he grew more lyrical. Neither were especially kind or wise, but you don't need wisdom and kindness to be a genius. More than a few have been thieves or murderers and died because of their violent natures. A genius doesn't need a mature moral character; he needs to blow his horn at least six hours a day. It's the "geniuses" with damaged characters and fucked-up stories of lives ill-spent that catch our fancy, while those occupying lesser places in jazz and who've suffered more mundane losses go unnoticed. I find Barry worth writing about, not because his is a cautionary tale, but because he plays beautifully despite not making it big.

Once after a gig and in a snow storm, our bass player invited him to stay at his home and wait for the storm to blow over. The man had gotten a full-time job at a local college after years of hustling gigs, and he belittled Barry for devoting himself so completely, so passionately, to his music. He took him around his new place, showing it off.

"Look at you," the guy unbelievably said. "Sure you play good, you're great, but shit, what do you have to show for it?"

Barry told me that story several times—it was an indignity you couldn't forget. The guy was one of the more talented musicians in Vermont, but we'd never heard him compliment anyone for his playing; because there was no longer fun in it for him. He had to take the fun out of it for anybody else. I wonder if that kind of bitterness doesn't go with the territory. It resides in rural districts inhabited by rusticated types who've "not quite reached their potential." I've noticed it in colleagues at the college where I used to teach and in musicians I know. And I've seen it in myself. But Barry is hard to read. He's full of half-ass stories about drugged and liquored-up musicians in crisis, nonstop stories that wall him off and make him opaque to anyone but himself.

For me all that remains of him is the clarity, the painful clarity, of his music.

On Happiness

≈

S O HERE I WAS, driving east over the Green
Mountains to an AA meeting in the village of
Lowell, thinking about my students in their
own puddles of final exam-induced unhappiness, and
the wild apple trees alongside the road were in violent
white bloom, and Burnt and Haystack Mountains
were misted over with early spring. The rutted dirt
road dipped into the valley, and for a moment, my
mental fog lifted off. I was in Hazen's Notch where
the foothills fold into shaggy crags and the horizon
closes up till you see nothing but a swatch of sky.
Moments later, I pulled into the St. Isidore parking
lot. I saw my logger buddies Phil and Rene smoking
outside in the last daylight, and gave them the high
sign and went inside where my old friend Ginny with

her liter of Diet Pepsi and Jon and Stub beside her grinned up at me.

Phil sat down at the head of the table—the chair for tonight—and announced the night's discussion topic: Regret. Phil opined Regret came from abandoning love. Regret with a capital "R," which becomes Remorse if we don't address our complacency.

In a few short minutes, my glum mood took a vacation.

A rough-looking guy I knew from years ago came in. He'd recently "gone back out" and was again in recovery. Somebody read the AA Preamble, and then the guy told the story of his first drunk and his first time in jail. When his voice rose in anger, I knew how he felt, that the anger was killing him. He regretted the people he'd hurt, and was angry that they'd let him hurt them. For years he'd had his own auto-body shop and breathed in enough fumes from the polymers to kill three of him. Before he quit drinking the first time, he drank in the afternoon. At night he went home to his trailer and his father, who was a bedridden diabetic alcoholic. The old man was on life-support, oxygen tubes hooked up to his nose, IV in his arm, and he was still drinking. There was nothing special about what the man said save that, after years taking care of his father, emptying his commode, bathing and changing him, it didn't matter to him if his father lived or died.

When I left the meeting, the man's words still rang in my head: I completely identified with him. Up the mountain a ways, I pulled over and looked down the moonlit valley. It was a late-spring night, but the trees this high up hadn't begun to leaf out. For at least an hour, I parked there out in the dark, thinking about my own father, who died on the last day of January of this year. A few days after his death, our spring box froze up in the coldest weather we'd experienced in Vermont. We had a chimney fire later that week and our pipes froze, which distracted me from the old man's death and caused me to sink into a numbing funk. I questioned the depths of my affection for the old man. Had I ever felt any real emotion toward him—positive or negative?

Coleridge, in his great gloomy Ode, says—
And those thin clouds above, in flakes and bars,
That give away their motion to the stars;
Those stars, that glide behind them or between,
Now sparkling, now bedimmed, but always seen:
Yon crescent Moon, as fixed as if it grew
In its own cloudless, starless lake of blue;
I see them all so excellently fair,
I see, not feel, how beautiful they are!

Recalling the poem now, I realized that my own un-happiness came from my inability to feel anything. Coleridge implies that dejection isn't sadness, it comes from other quarters.

In the second stanza of his "Dejection Ode," he admits he can't "lift the smothering weight from off (his) breast," and

Though I should gaze for ever
On that green light that lingers in the west:
I may not hope from outward forms to win
The passion and the life, whose fountains are
    within.

I'd like to think Coleridge's inability "to lift that smothering weight" was a momentary stop on the way to feeling something. From what I know of him, he felt nothing more than not, and such an emotional emptiness helped along by his opium habit caused a creative aridity that made his poetry dry up.

I was moved by Coleridge's realization the "fountains" of feeling were within —unobtainable, yet so visible:

I see them all so excellently fair
I see, not feel, how beautiful they are !

The paradox is that the poem expresses a state of being that contains both a lack of feeling and a capacity to experience loss. The speaker's dejection is not triggered, as it might be today, by external events—it is not *provoked*. It just IS. The self is to blame for the dejection the speaker feels, not what he reads in the newspapers.

After the numbness descends, the cold creeps in through the wall cracks, you sit by the fire with the wood stove cranked, and are you're still cold.

∽

My wife and I had been there at the rest home when my father died. It had begun to snow, the radio said a storm was coming, and I wanted to drive home before it arrived. My father's death was unremarkable. He went into breathing spasms, not breathing and then breathing, and he clenched my hand, then let it go. I thought it would be a kindness if he passed away, and then his eyes closed and he opened them, and for a moment it felt as though he recognized me. The afternoon went on like that until just before dark, when he stopped breathing again. I felt an icy calmness. I counted to ten, and then he was gone for good.

I pulled him up out of the pillows and hugged him, and I don't know if I felt anything, but something in me was programmed to give a shriek as I let him go.

Back in the cabin, I called my sister and gave her the news. She sounded very far away. She'd been up from New York to visit my father a week before, the first time she'd come since we'd moved him to Vermont. I hadn't offered to put her up at our house, because we had lost our running water in the last freeze and had no plumbing. Like me and my father, she was a drinker, a sore spot between us, and she had spent that night in a motel. When she had arrived (drunk, I was later told) at the rest home next morning, I made sure I wasn't there.

I hung up the phone and turned to my wife, who'd been crying while all I'd been capable of was anger at my sister. I didn't feel sad. At a certain age you fall into death as my father did, pulling with you a train of half-fulfilled obligations. While in the weeks leading up to my father's death, I hadn't the time to think about these things, as I walked to the outhouse that night it was snowing, the hemlock bows bent down with it, and I felt numb. I hadn't used the outhouse in years, but with the pipes froze up after two forty-below nights, I had an excuse: I sat there, my trousers and long johns to my knees, looking out through the branches to our snow-covered pond, and for a moment the numbness lifted off. I felt happy.

The rewards of a late-night trek are constitutional and spiritual. On a clear January night, the sky ignites with shooting stars, and galaxies you've never seen before burn through the screen of trees above the outhouse, tearing another asshole out of the roof of your skull. My father's death numbed me and made me alive: that's what confused me. Walking from the privy to the brook to fetch water, I could tell how cold it was by the texture and squeak of the snow. I heard the brook ruminating beneath the snow and ice, and savored the thwack of my axe as I chopped down to the pool I'd dammed up between a pair of boulders the fall before.

That evening deer had come down to drink and had broken through the skin of ice on the hole I'd chopped, and I saw their tracks leading up the ravine. At dawn, as I fell off to sleep, I heard the snow grains dinging the roof. Thence followed a morning of restless dreams of the rickety old mansion where my father had spent the last months of his life. I wandered around its corridors looking for him, and everything was the same save that he was gone. I awoke in our bedroom to blinding snow outside my window, and my mind took an excursion to the place I'd dreamed about where my father had spent the last two years of his life.

⌒

Red Stone had been built from pink Italian marble. It had a slate roof, high gables and a wide porch from where you looked down to the Lake Champlain islands. Inside, above the mantle, hung an inscription from Ovid written in Latin, that said, "Perhaps someday we'll remember these things with pleasure." The fireplace below the inscription was flanked by paint-chipped columns that enhanced the decayed mood of the place. The mansion had been built by a doctor before the Civil War. The quote from Ovid reflected on the happy years of the doctor's life, but its meaning had reversed itself after the mansion had been turned into an old-age home. Most of the folks at Red Stone had some form of dementia, and the irony of Ovid's quote was that they couldn't remember anything.

Each time I came to visit my old man, I stopped before the great fireplace to read the inscription. But the last I saw of him before he lost any semblance of coherence, knowing he was in bad shape, I rushed past the fireplace to his room where he was tied down in a wheelchair so he couldn't "act out" as he had recently with the staff. He looked pleased to see me, and he called me "Ernie." Ernie was an old reprobate drinking friend from his life on Long Island. "Hey Ernie," he said, "how's it hangin'?"

~

During my worst drinking days when I looked in the mirror, I saw my father's sidelong glance bent on getting another drink. Increasingly, I saw myself in people who were new to recovery, telling me what they thought were unique stories but were variations on the theme of drinking and shame, stories of parents and grandparents drinking that ended in either recovery or decline, in indifference to death or a violent embrace of it. I preferred to think that what I loved and hated about these people was the dark vitality that took them over. Even after many years sober, they felt it tugging and drawing them closer to death.

On this particular visit, in the month before my father's death, I got foolishly—unreasonably—angry with him. I wasn't Ernie!

I should have been touched by his flashback to his old friend, but I exclaimed that I was in a hurry, and rushed out to the parking lot, and got into my Subaru where my dog was waiting. I thought I saw my father's wheel-chaired profile through the huge bay window. Then I backed into a dumpster at the edge of the parking lot, and felt the crunch, and heard the tinkling glass. I leaned against the wheel, my dog's kisses sloppy-warm on my cheek. My father waved, I thought at me (now I realize it was another useless gesture, but that was the image I had of him), and I took a turn on a road I'd rarely traveled, driving fast, the river running high beside the road, the dog yipping as the road turned to mud track. I felt a sudden elation—the same burst of elation I'm feeling now. A few Holsteins ambled along. A tail-wind smattered the broken rear window, and then came the sleet and rain. I stumbled out of the car, in high spirits. Red Dog ran into a cornfield and rolled in the fresh manure.

Then he barked into the sleety wind.

Which would be the end of it, if not for an idea that struck as I turned toward the river. I saw my little retriever bounding along the river's edge, rapids and still water, a turbulent millrace of riffles and then the ragged sweep of it all, and it came to me I didn't have to be unhappy. I whistled for the dog, and he lifted his snoot with such happiness that my next thought was succinct as an equation. I walked awhile and crossed an iron bridge where two kids were fishing and glanced down at the river and up to the hills and the lolling clouds, where a charged and driven force was hauled up and thrown down by a virgin idea. Ideas of mortality and transitoriness, trepidation, and doubt all peeled away to reveal the tender under-skin of the absolute. A truck hurtled along, rattling the pylons.

The dog panted beside me. I tromped into darkness behind my dog, and as the woods beyond the river folded over us, frog eggs glistened in the snow melt. In the afterglow of my happiness, a din of gnats and mayflies rose up.

⤸

My father's memory and health deteriorated even more. Each Sunday when I visited Red Stone, I saw new signs of decline. He became incontinent and no longer walked even from his room to the dining hall, but was confined all day to the wheelchair. He was disdainful and indifferent toward my wife and me, and as mud-season turned into a very cold spring, he went beyond indifference into a kind of unknowingness. Who knows what the relationship is between my father's decline and my unjustified happiness—though I had reason not to care about him as much as most sons might care about their dads—but let's say a door opened in my life, a door that hung on the hinges of grief.

I didn't know how I could possibly be happy, but it came, and I thought hard on it. It came during the next eight months in swoops and eddies in a giddiness following his death.

That giddiness went along with my early sobriety, and I'm afraid with late-sobriety, too. Known in AA as a "pink cloud," it's often followed by the cumulus of depression. Not only the newly sober fall off pink clouds. The challenge is to separate joy from hyper-mania. My model for true happiness is Red Dog, retriever of all retrievers. He's got a thickly layered golden coat, tough webbed feet and a muscular little body. A superb athlete, he'll fetch for you till your arm falls off. He's not a contemplative dog: his idea of fun isn't lying by a cozy fire dreaming of far-away summers. He's an action-dog. A fly-by-the-seat-of-your-pants dog. A heat-seeking missile of a dog. Happy isn't the right word to describe him when he's in motion: joy is more like it. He is joyful if he's got a stick or a ball to chase or a creek to swim across. If Red Dog was black, I'd call him Black Muzzle, the dog in this poem by the great S'ung Dynasty poet, Su Tung-P'o, translated by Burton Watson:

Black Muzzle
When I came to Tan-chou, I acquired a watchdog named Black Muzzle. He was very fierce, but soon got used to people. He went with me to Ho-p'u, and when we passed Ch'eng-mai, he startled everyone by swimming across the river. So as a joke I wrote this poem for him.

Black Muzzle, south sea dog,
how lucky I am to be your master!
On scraps growing plump as a gourd,
never grumbling for fancier food.
Gentle by day, you learn to tell my friends;
ferocious by night, you guard the gate.
When I told you I was going back north,
you wagged your tail and danced with delight,

bounced along after the boy,
tongue out, dripping a shower of sweat.
You wouldn't go by the long bridge
but took a short cut across the clear deep bay,
scrambling up the bank fiercer than a tiger.
You steal meat—a fault, though a minor one,
but I'll spare the whip this time.
You nod your head by way of thanks,
Heaven having given you no words.
Someday I'll get you to take a letter home—
Yellow Ears was your ancestor, I'm sure.

On one level, "Black Muzzle" may be read as an
expression of the poet's joy at hearing he's soon to
be released from his exile on Hainan Island off the
south coast of China, where he's been relegated to a
minor post. Burton Watson tells us in his translator's
notes to the poem: "This year the poet was ordered
to leave Tan-chou and go to Ho-p'u in Lien-chou
on the mainland opposite Hainan, the first sign that
the worst of his exile was over. Ch'eng-mai is on the
north coast of Hainan, near where the poet took the
boat to the mainland."

While there's no attempt in Su's poem to human-
ize his dog, Black Muzzle shares his joy openly with
his master. He isn't a coddled lap dog, but a center of
vital impulses; he leaps into the water with such elan
that the poet has to forgive his craziness. In fact, the
poet is moved to compare him to the legendary dog
"Yellow Ears."

There's something regal, imperial even, about Black Muzzle. The writing's so turbulently alive, I'm caught in the loving irreverence shared by master and dog. When I think of the Zen spirit, this poem's lash of energy, its dazzling detail, always comes to mind. All this is knocked off jauntily, nonchalantly: the water droplets spattered from the dog's muzzle are like ink splashes from a calligrapher's pen.

During my own dog's most brilliant moments, when he's drunk with delight and bursts into my life, I know what it is to be an animal stoned-out in the wild. Animals get drunk more often than you'd think. Deer get themselves tipsy on late-season apples. In September, bears carouse in the blackberries behind our house, while in late winter, cedar waxwings bomb-out on fermented chokecherries and fly into my study window.

There's a wild goat that climbs the Rockies to eat a weed which flourishes only at extreme altitudes. The weed makes the goat high. After he eats his full, he'll stand bug-eyed on the mountain and take in the stupendous view. He's not just savoring the "high"—he's filled with goat-wonder.

Animals get stoned when their drugs of choice are in season and when they need an altered reality—at the end of summer after berries and apples have fermented and they're ready to go into hibernation, or in deep winter when they need a reprieve from the cold.

My own way of coping with winter used to be

just as extreme: I'd sit in my car, drain one beer after
another, and more times than not, fall asleep and wake
up with cigarette burns on my jacket. Luckily, there
were no dents in my car, no unexplained scratches or
bruises on my body the next morning. A light snow
might have fallen, and through the leafless trees the
entire mountainside sparkled, and I'd open another
beer, stand outside for a few minutes. Once the car
stalled out on another dirt road. At twenty-below just
after a heavy snow, I fell asleep. After I woke up, my
fingers and toes in the first stages of frostbite, I hoofed
it to a cabin where a light was on. They were drunk
in there, too—a party was going on—and they asked
me in and handed me a beer, and I kept on drinking
until dawn.

⤶

Now, on this inaugural evening in early Spring after
my father's death, I start up the car, shift into low
gear, and glide the last three miles down the mountain through Hazen's Notch. At home, I tell my wife
about the guy at the meeting, how he'd taken care
of his diabetic father, and had begun drinking again.
And it reminded you of your father, she says. We're
standing on the deck, the mist has cleared, the Big
Dipper arcs above the hemlocks, and I think of my
father, buried alongside my mother in a Connecticut
graveyard. He never got sober, yet lived to the hallu-
cinated old age of eighty-seven.

Two weeks later I find myself heading back over
the mountains to Lowell, where I sit facing my alky

friends. A few old timers come in, there's a burst of laughter, and the meeting starts. The subject tonight is "keeping the memory fresh." A guy describes a panic attack he had back in the winter, how he was down on the floor pounding the carpet. He craved a drink, and then the desire just lifted off; but he still had to push through the fear. My own panic attacks have been no less serious. Just before I first came here, I'd gone to rehab and attended AA meetings, and learned some basic AA principles and slogans. But it took at least a year to realize how hopeless I was.

Lowell opened up just after the last time I got sober so many years ago. I've seen miracles performed and disasters averted, fools made if not into saints, then into people who function "normally." The meeting is hard to get to in the winter: the mountain roads often are clotted with snow, but in late spring we'll remark on the beauty of the rolling meadows and a grove of budding sugar maples behind the church, while curious kids on beat-up bicycles and a few stray dogs check out us troubled souls.

～

Who is this Su Tung-P'o, the author of "Black Muzzle," and why does he mean so much to me? Like most Chinese poets, he was a government official, in his case an important administrator sent to jail and relegated more than once to obscure posts for his political views. Among a nation of calligraphers, he's the most textured and visual of poets, traversing the

"Middle Way," balancing the virtues of friendship and solitude, regret and optimism.

What an odd state of affairs for the poets of old China: they were hermits, but sociable ones, always willing to tip a cup of wine with a friend.

Su Tung-P'o writes:

This outing of ours never had a purpose;
let the lone boat swing about as it will.
In the middle of the current, lying face up,
I greet the breeze that happens along
and lift a cup to offer to the vastness:
How pleasant that we have not thought of each
    other!
Coming back through two river valleys,
clouds and water shine in the night.

Motion is the key for me here, motion and stillness, as is any venture into the unknowable. The boat swings about and the breeze blows, while the poet is caught up in a picture larger than the one of him and the boat. Though he seems alone, there's reference to a friend who may be no more than us, his Reader. Though Su has set out in his boat with a companion for a night of lotus-viewing, he's adrift in a "lone boat" and doesn't care where he's going. His lonely voyage touches me—it has no "purpose" but to experience the "vastness," unanchored out among the stars.

I've failed to say much about this semester's classes. A woman in her late-twenties wrote a remarkable piece about "edible" Chinese poetry, citing poems where food is mentioned—bamboo shoots and rice for the poor, kumquats and camel's hoof soup for the rich. She went deeper into the poems, examining how food is doled out when there isn't much to go around, and how it is shared and celebrated with a cup of tea or wine with a friend. She discussed those poems as repasts in themselves and showed how their presentation, much of the time alongside a painting, resembles the presentation of food in China.

The poems, she writes, are meant to be read aloud as offerings to friends, spiritual nourishment.

But more essays need grading. They get mixed reviews. The best are close analyses of poems, the worst a slurry of off-hand, first-draft stabs in the dark.

The semester wears on. Though my father has been gone a few months, he seems far away—more distant than then the recent dead should be. On Graduation Day, I cheer on our crew of young scholars beneath a white tent on the campus green. The sky is an ocean-deep blue. Red and white pennants snap and ripple like prayer flags in the wind off the mountains.

EPILOGUE:
BORDER CROSSING

~~

I'M DRIVING THROUGH the Cold Hollow
Mountains near my Vermont home one evening
with my friend Jacques and two others, to an AA
meeting in the town of Montgomery, and as we round
a bend a moose plunges out of the bushes. I brake
just a few feet from disaster and kill the engine. The
moose turns its bearded head toward the four of us in
my car. His body is slathered with mud from rolling in
the muck to ward off deer flies. He dips his maw into
the ditch, and you can hear his ruminative munching,
his meaty shanks sucking mud. I know a number of
folks who've hit moose, including a former student
who slammed into one on the interstate whose kids
were saved by the reinforced-steel body of her Volvo,
and another guy who hit one near Jacques' place, the
moose landing in a mess of smashed windshield and

moose shit in his lap. Can't say how often I've braked
for a moose sidling out of the night as determined to
barge into me as I am to avoid him. "Ever smell a bull
moose in the rut?" Jacques says. "They dig a hole a
few feet deep, piss and roll in it till they stink so bad a
cow'll catch his scent a mile off."

The parking lot at St. Isidore's in Montgomery
adjoins a noisy frog pond, and tonight the peepers
and bullfrogs are gut-deep and throaty. I'm more than
a few years sober, but I still have an exalted feeling
when the four of us arrive at St. Katherine's. It's cool
and damp in the basement. On the wall hang AA
slogans—ONE DAY AT A TIME, KEEP IT SIMPLE,
LET GO AND LET GOD—beside faded prints of
anonymous Catholic saints. There's a smell of bad
coffee, a backed-up septic system, and stale sweat.
Jacques sits at the end of the table, and I take a seat
between him and the Abenaki woman I'll call
Yvonne, who came with us.

Before the meeting commences, Yvonne tells us
she's going to have triplets and has been drinking since
last weekend. She was at a Fourth of July powwow
at the chief's house, and the tribe was celebrating
by pouring gasoline over a couple of wrecked cars
and blowing them up. She started with a little wine,
graduated to harder stuff, and when she came-to that
blackout weekend, she found herself in a sleeping bag
with a Mohawk she'd never met two hundred miles
north in Quebec.

"I'm ashamed to say he was a Mohawk," she grins.

At this point in my sobriety, I usually try to let the newer guys talk, but tonight I tell my own recovery story.

I'm on the road somewhere in Vermont: it's pelting snow, my car goes into a greasy spin sending me into a tumbledown barn, and I'm coming out of a blackout with no idea where I've been or where I'm headed—all I know is I have to pee like hell and I'm craving another drink. Then I'm sitting inside the empty barn with another drunk, an older guy with a handlebar mustache and a bloody gash on his forehead slumped on a hay bale beside me and we're talking about women we've never had—women we couldn't have had we were so drunk—and I know this is crazy though no crazier than the other experiences I've had.

"That's my story," I say. "But I still don't know where I was going that night."

"Maybe nowheres," puts in a guy named Teddy who seems fed up with the silence he's walled himself into. "The hardest thing about losing someone to drink," he says, referring to a recently deceased childhood friend who had relapsed, "is that while they were alive they weren't aware of you and could've thought less about what you thought about their drinking. You may not sign on to their view, which makes little difference as they are not of this world, and you're not either."

Ignoring Teddy, I say that after my "last drunk," I went to rehab and got sober, but the following years were a mixed blessing. A few drinking memories were readily accessible, but the most harrowing and painful were buried in denial. Misery loves company, I suppose, and drunks like Jacques and Yvonne and Teddy have helped me confront my past by sharing their yarns—most of which involve car accidents.

"I'd get up in the morning,' says Jacques, "and I'd go out to my car to see if there was any blood on it or if I'd piled into the mailbox. Finally, I got sick and tired of being sick and tired." He frowns and takes a slug of coffee, and like so many times before, he lurches into how he'd leave his job at Ben & Jerry's Ice Cream plant in Waterbury and head for a bar on the lake to drink till five in the morning with other Ben & Jerry's guys, and drive home in time to greet his long-suffering wife who'd send him half-plastered back to work. On our way home, I want to tell Jacques I've heard his tale so many times from him I could recite it chapter-and-verse, but I won't hurt his feelings. His stories used to move me to tears, but I've heard them so much, they've lost emotion, and are honed into skeletal fragments of his past.

↜

The best AA storytellers are not always exemplary AA'ers, but their knack for tale-telling and stimulating introspection helps others in fresh recovery. The most effective speakers are often new in the Program—by keeping things alive, they trigger forgotten or glossed-over memories in the rest of us—but Old Timers like me and Jacques stumble through our stories, not so much shy as reticent to share our drinking past. Addiction "experts" believe some folks go through PTSD by telling our stories year after year, that after our wounds are exposed to fresh air, they need time to heal. But revisiting our past night after night and exposing our folly, we reopen old scars to where they're permanently infected: fear overcomes us, nightmares ensue, and the past we struggled to reconcile ourselves to haunts us.

Recently I found myself trembling as I retold my "last drunk" story. Others may have noticed before I did, but were kind enough to say nothing. On the way home, I brought all this up to Jacques, and he said the same thing had happened to him last year. Once he found himself unable to talk. Outwardly, things went well for him, but telling his story gave him little comfort: we both dreaded speaking at meetings and, what's more, the prospect of hearing others "qualify" pained us.

Jacques and I knew many old timers who'd quit AA and had relapsed, suggesting that straying from the Program even after years of sobriety courted disaster—so out of fear we stuck with it. But aside from their drunk-alogues, I knew little about other guys. They'd smoothed out their stories till much of what they said was peppered with AA clichés.

I myself had honed down my story, getting out the kinks till the mindless ritual bored me and, no doubt, the rest of us.

Nothing in the Big Book and in the Twelve Steps addresses this issue—if indeed it *is* an issue. The AA founders wrote the Big Book and The Steps when they were no more than a decade sober and couldn't anticipate the challenges of late sobriety. The Twelve Steps charted a path of early recovery, focusing on how newcomers achieve and sustain it, but after a decade or two hearing recovery narratives and telling our stories, guys like Jacques and me have hit a massive roadblock.

⤳

It's not for nothing that Bob Smith and Bill Wilson, AA's founding fathers, were from Vermont, where six-month winters turn people to drink. Both expressed complementary aspects of the Puritan character, Doctor Bob with his homespun "keep things stupid, Stupid" and Bill Wilson with his knack—as a Madison Avenue man—for translating complex ideas into Rotarian language. In keeping with their Calvinist mindset, they believed a drunk could not cure himself, but staved off suffering day-by-day. Salvation— sobriety—was provisional. Once off the sauce, a drunk avoided suffering by realizing, through the Twelve Steps, his fallen nature and that he was powerless over alcohol. By "turning things over to God, " abjectly confessing his faults to another, and making amends to those he'd wronged, including himself, a recovering drunk might stay sober. Yet these steps didn't guarantee permanent recovery; an exemplary AA'er might stumble because the "happy road to recovery" is fraught with temptation. In a weaker moment he might turn away from God and give in to the Self.

The AA philosophy is fraught with contradictions. Bill and Bob warned against over-thinking, but their path involved a kind of mental hair-splitting that verged on the metaphysical. You're told to avoid the "pink cloud" that's often followed by depression and also coaxed to maintain a beatific "serenity." While AA's Twelve Steps are "suggested," in practice beginners are instructed not to avoid them. You need not believe in a Higher Power to get started, but are scolded for trying to find an "easier, softer way." The contradictions of AA philosophy—the dialectic of a humanistic gentleness and Puritan rigor—are hard to reconcile with the success of AA over other paths to recovery.

Maybe the tension exerted by these contradictions is self-corrective—you can't get too complacent or too vigilant—but they're also symptomatic of AA double-think. We're bombarded with before-and-after tales of spiritual transformation that resemble bible-meeting testimonials: an AA story revolves around ritualistic once-I-was-lost, now-I'm-found stories of shame and redemption, and The Twelve Steps reinforce the narrative by encouraging a thorough "moral inventory" and "making amends to those we have wronged." Whether or not we're forgiven isn't as important as asking for it: making amends is an end in itself and doesn't require empathy toward the person we've hurt. I've found little in the literature about forgiveness—we want absolution, not forgiveness, and absolution doesn't erase the pain we've caused others, apologies notwithstanding.

When I entered the Program, this approach provided a model for recovery. The Fourth Step, suggesting a "thorough moral inventory," made me examine my life as a drunk and to look at my past as a mess, the present as a provisional paradise. I went through years abstaining, but I knew I'd drink again. I drank through college, graduate school, teaching, and writing jobs. I humiliated girlfriends and best friends. My drinking injuries included a broken jaw, a cracked skull, a broken ankle from fights I provoked in Paris and Madrid, on the Isle of Mallorca and in Mexico City, and Shanghai.

⌒

I'm on leaf-strewn patio of Ray W's place in Guanajuato, Mexico, the ruins of last night strewn before us. And I'm still drinking. That's what I remember of that morning, aside from the fact we just heard on the radio that Bobby Kennedy had just been shot. "You exchange one shame for less shame," Ray says, squinting past me to some nameless local who's just joined us. My wife, Suzanne, is here too. She's down with a bug she picked up at a taco stand in Monterrey—her fever's up to a hundred-and-two, but a cold shower hasn't brought her temp down. She hears the news through the open window and races to join us. My God, we say in unison, RFK's been shot. We drank through the first Kennedy assassination and the Martin Luther King assassination, and now we're drunk in the mountains of central Mexico the morning after Bobby Kennedy has been shot. Suzanne collapses into a patio chair, her face blotched by fever, but I pay her no mind. Ray W.'s Mexican wife Nellie pours another mescal—I remember the half-empty bottle with a little red worm at the bottom and the word GUSANO ROJO printed on the side—and I don't slam it down, but say to myself, you're drinking the acrid essence of Mexico the day after Bobby Kennedy has been shot. The mescal goes down straight and smooth, then explodes back into my mouth with bile. I excuse myself to puke into the prickly pears. A dust devil makes its way up the valley, and I'm high on the fumes of my own puke, so drunk I can't see my wife's deathly ill.

Ray's memory of when we heard RFK was shot is unlike mine. As he remembers it, he's driving through Mexico City to pick up a former writing teacher at the airport. On almost every street corner, trench-coated dudes are pretending to be reading newspapers, standing alongside Mexican army guys armed to the teeth. The American radio station from Texas fades in and out, so the news is sketchy, but it is clear RFK's been tragically shot. The airport is filled with more plainclothesmen reading American newspapers—obviously something's afoot, and Ray's paranoid lights blaze on. For the sake of narrative coherence, he's drunk: after he picks up his former poetry teacher, he and the teacher, the poet John Logan, head to a close-by airport bar and proceed to get so loaded they can't find Ray's VW in the huge parking lot.

Logan's best known for a lengthy poem called "A Trip to Four or Five Towns," a few lines I quote from here:

> In New York I got drunk, to tell the truth,
> And almost got locked up when a beat
> friend with me took a leak in a telephone
>   booth ... Oh, if I mock,
> it is without heart, I thought
> of the torn limbs of Orpheus
> scattered in the grass on the hills of Thrace.
> Do poets have to have such trouble with the
>   female race?

Driving out of Mexico City, Nellie at his side and Logan in the back seat deeply drunk, they come on a roadblock manned by two Guardia and a gringo in sunglasses and a trench coat who wave them through. They drive through miles of breathtakingly beautiful Mexican countryside, and when they reach Ray's rented villa in Guanajuato, they're ready to start drinking again.

Our two stories of that morning, Ray's and mine, underscore how untrustworthy a drunk's memory is.

For one thing, nothing in mine rhymes. What matters is that we lay out the memory and autopsy it till it's no longer a rotting corpse, but a dried-up cadaver of our drinking past. That's the routine AA recommends on how to deal with this stuff. Does it matter that when I retrieve that memory—it seems cauterized into my unconscious—that a shiver of guilt and revulsion goes through me?

I bring up these two versions of that morning in 1968 because just a day ago I got a call on my cell from Ray as I pulled into an Episcopal Church for an AA meeting. Ray and I have kept in close touch over the years. The meeting was about to start, but we had time to talk. I said I'd been thinking of that morning and wanted to write about it as part of a "Fourth Step" Did he recall it? He laughed at my misremembering so completely. On a conscious level, I agreed that Ray's story was indeed more persuasive, more replete with details, than mine, but I still can't accept on an internal level anything but my own recollection.

One of us has a false memory of what happened the day after RFK was shot, but what difference does it make? Much if not most of our lives—our drinking lives—is misremembered, left a free-floating, object-less fear that lurks inside us. My memory of that day continues with me in a horrendous argument with Suzanne and smashing a ceramic-tile coffee table, but I've no idea what we were fighting about—if indeed we did fight. I see her moaning and crying, she's got a bad case of Montezuma's Revenge . . . and then I'm

heading out the door to God knows where—and the
memory fades.

⤳

Many meetings I go to are dominated by old timers
who hold chapter and verse to the Steps and the Big
Book, while others with flexible approaches to recovery keep their own buttoned-up counsel. This is not
to say everyone in late sobriety is dissatisfied with the
Program—it's crusty old AA fanatics who most often
set agendas and discourage dynamic discussions and
argument. We're not a debating society, and in early
recovery, we need a roadmap to stay sober, but after
years in AA, many of us look from the past to the
future. How do we renew our sobriety and what are
our core beliefs?

The word "serenity" is often used to describe
the mental and spiritual condition we're aiming
for—a condition not unlike the state of "Clear" in
Scientology. In both AA and Scientology, the expression and consequent release of a previously repressed
emotion, achieved through reliving the experience
that caused it, is the goal. But what happens after we've
reached our goal? In AA, serenity's often equated—
and confused, I think—with a kind of spiritual stasis.
Now that we've achieved that godlike state, where do
we go from here?

Some of us don't believe in God, but still manage
to stay sober. In recent years, a few agnostic AA meetings have cropped up, but they're a precious few. Most

meetings discourage "an easier, softer (and agnostic) way"—and turn off folks with alternative spiritual views—sending more than a few packing.

After nearly three decades, I'm reinventing my Program. How do I grow out of my addiction and become a more realized person? I must choose either to stay in AA and practice The Steps as prescribed, to quit going to meetings and strike out on my own, or to stick with AA and advocate for change.

⤳

Some years ago, I chaired a meeting with an Anglican priest (a staunch believer), and we asked what was new in everyone's world. We discouraged talk about drinking. We wanted to know about everyone's hobbies and their past-times. What made them happy? What had they done to enrich their lives?—and we were amazed at their stories. One woman said she'd rediscovered dancing—after she quit drinking, she'd taken up ballet again—and another fellow I'd known for years told about a furniture-making hobby he'd made into a lucrative business. I'd begun painting and had included my watercolors in a book of poems I published.

I'm sad that the tone of that meeting didn't carry over to other ones.

But so it goes. Was there here a more uplifting way to sustain my sobriety after all these years?

⤳

My own past still has a tenacious hold on me. For years I worked as a musician, playing trombone in jazz groups in northern New England, making a fool of myself onstage and off, and still I drank. Once while playing in Montreal, I'd taken some kind of awful drug a hatcheck girl had given me, and half-way through the first set, things didn't add up, the other cats started looking like cats, and so on. This wasn't the '60's and I was no longer my blazing for-mer jazz-self, but had reverted to the regimen of the ancestors—snifter of schnapps for breakfast, a cocktail before noon, and now that drug she had given me. Nothing distinguished that bar from any other but its name, Green Dolphin Street—the band had dubbed Purple Porpoise Alley, ha-ha.

"Take me home with you," she said after the gig, and I said I was married, and besides, I had no home to go to, which was a lie. I'd lied earlier at the bor-der crossing that the purpose of my visit was to play music with a group of Montrealers and that I'd not be making money. I lied to myself about the drugs and alcohol and how I planned to get sober: I had no plan. And I lied about where my career as a writer and a musician was going. Maybe I'd played well tonight and impressed the other musicians with my skills as a trombonist, but I've no idea if that was true.

I got in my car after the gig, the night's music still blowing through my head, and crossed the bridge from Montreal into Quebec's Eastern Townships, my mind spinning from drugs and booze, my hands fastened to the wheel like snakes. I headed south toward Vermont, and in a confused state, I stopped at an all-night convenience store and asked where I was. Beyond some outbuildings, bulrushes sighed and rustled in the rain, and more distant, the glow of the meat-packing plants of a ville called Saint Luc. The clerk said, just keep going, you can't miss Sutton, where I'd find the border crossing, so I headed south, my horn strapped like a corpse to the car roof. At midnight, as I approached the Vermont crossing, lightning flickered along a river and the customs station was brightly lit to catch any crime. As I crossed the river bridge, a monkey—yes, a monkey!—scrambled from the bushes in flight from here to them, my God, a monkey in these latitudes, and when I told the border guard (who wasn't impressed), I was made to get out of the car. I've no memory of what happened after that. Let's say I returned home, my car blessedly unscathed, and that my wife and I had words. I vowed to get help for my "problem."

It's quarter to seven of a summer evening in Darby Falls, Vermont, and a group of Old Timers are chatting around a defunct fountain in the town park, our words softened by a warm south breeze. We're old and new timers, and we know each other intimately. Someone's practicing piano scales nearby, and under the shade of some turning maples and a darkening evening sky, the lights of the Methodist church pattern against the leaves. Tonight feels different, but it shouldn't. We're always in mourning, folks come and go, they get sober and quietly exit our lives as Jon Z did last week. John was an alcohol counselor and a veteran bird watcher, an amateur historian and a brilliant nature photographer. He also suffered from an anxiety that never left him, despite the wisdom he shared with others; but as co-sponsors, we saw each other through good and bad.

Jon and I talked lots about The Higher Power (I hope his God, whoever he or she might be is with him now). When we entered the Program, we were agnostics: the concept of an all-powerful Christian God offended us and had nothing to do with our lives. But desperate times require desperate measures, and what did we have to lose?

God might not exist, but believing in Him, we both decided, might help us stay sober.

All of which leads me to another night, and another snowy night in Vermont, when Jon and I had our "mystical experience." At the close of an especially moving Third Step session, we all held hands as we began the Lord's Prayer, and a chorus of voices filled the room. They sounded like they'd come from the church basement walls. They were in a foreign language—Hebrew? Aramaic?—that blotted out our words. We kept reciting the prayer like nothing weird had happened while the voices chanted on. For a moment, I thought we'd broken into glossolalia—that we were speaking in tongues. I made out individual words, but they made no sense. We finished the Prayer and the chanting stopped abruptly, and we were more or less speechless. The reaction of our group was as strange as the voices. We stood around in silence; there was little to say but "Whaddya know?" "That was really weird, weren't it?" and "How about that?" as we put on our winter coats and headed home.

Next week, in another church basement, a woman who'd been at that snowy meeting came up and said to me, "That really happened, didn't it?" and I replied, yes it had, and she shrugged and said "Well, isn't that something?" Of course, I was disturbed by that night: sober just a couple of years, I wondered was I going nuts?

I've come to realize that the "miracle" of the night wasn't what we'd heard, but that we were all sober. Still sober.

⌣

I'm still an agnostic, miracles and chimeras, drunk and sober visions notwithstanding. I'm not interested in heading down a believer's path, the one I'm following is clear of mystical detritus. Still, I need to be careful not to fall for an easy mysticism to handle my personal issues, some of which relate to drinking, others that don't. Things happen that can't be explained and don't want explanation. I'm heartened there's no AA literature about late sobriety, that the roadmap is fogged and uncharted. But I wonder what a Twelve Steps of Late Sobriety might look like. It's easy to say it'd be all positive, that the negative Thou Shalt Nots would all be removed. The positive ones, those that commend us to help others stay sober, would need including.

Am I being presumptuous?

Each step on this new path is fraught with over-thinking. The new path—a path of renewal—inspires me to see life before I got sober as rich with heart-break, that the wind blowing me toward self-destruc-tion contains promise. Even while I drank there were lovely moments—intoxicating moments—moments that defied categorizing. Now that I'm sober, I reach back into my past and fight against a repugnance to all that richness. I'm in my car at an unknown border crossing. I see the monkey cross the road before I reach the river, and I pause and say, "Whaddya know? Wasn't that something?"